HOW TO DO YOU

The Life Changing Art of Mastering Your Thoughts and Taking Control of Your Life

by Jacqueline Hurst

ABOUT THE AUTHOR

Jacqueline Hurst is one of the UK's leading life coaches and an expert in the wellness field. She is a teacher, speaker and ambassador with more than 15 years' experience. She is GQ Magazine's resident life coach and columnist, owner of the online coaching school, The Life Class, and a private practitioner with clients ranging from celebrities to CEOs. Over the years, she has worked with more than 7000 clients worldwide.

Jacqueline has helped many famous names to work through their most personal issues, including TV personality Greg Wallace, who she helped to overcome anxiety issues when he appeared on BBC's Strictly Come Dancing. Others include a well-known sportsman plagued by worries about losing his edge; a woman who had risen to become a business leader but had an utter dread of public speaking, and a top actor whose doctors had given him an ultimatum to give up smoking…

Jacqueline is regularly featured in the media as an expert in her field, including The Sunday Times, The Telegraph, Harper's Bazaar, Daily Mail, BBC News, BBC London Radio and the Oprah Winfrey Network. She also works with brands including Virgin, Nivea, Vitality Insurance, Estee Lauder, Space NK, Matches Fashion, Sweaty Betty, Lulu lemon and Bank of America. Jacqueline travels the world lecturing and seeing international clients, from Miami to Ibiza.

At a young age, Jacqueline became addicted to drugs, alcohol and amphetamines. She also suffered with anorexia and bulimia, and for ten years, her life spiralled out of control. After her second attempt at ending it all in her mid-twenties, she had a breakthrough moment, and with a lot of hard work, tenacity, courage and resilience, she managed to turn her life around. She embarked on a worldwide journey to educate herself about mental health in all its complexities, beginning her formal studies in neuro-linguistic programming (NLP) at the Bennett Stellar University in Miami. She went on to train in the 'Austin Method' of Advanced Structured Hypnotherapy in London and then at the prestigious Life Coach School.

In 2007, Jacqueline became a full-time life coach, qualified hypnotherapist and NLP and cognitive behavioural therapy (CBT) master practitioner. As important as her formal qualifications are, she regards her life experiences and intuition as key to her success, and has dedicated herself to helping others improve their lives beyond measure.

www.jacquelinehurst.com

www.thelifeclass.com

CONTENTS

INTRODUCTION: 6

CHAPTER ONE: 8

    MY LIFE STORY 8

CHAPTER TWO: 25

    HOW TO GAIN CONTROL OVER YOUR THOUGHTS AND ACTIONS: 25

CHAPTER THREE 43

    HOW TO BEAT ANXIETY 43

CHAPTER FOUR: 60

    HOW TO STOP FEELING STUCK 60

CHAPTER FIVE 77

    HOW TO STOP PROCRASTINATING 77

CHAPTER SIX: 95

    HOW TO MANAGE YOUR STRESS LEVELS AND FIND BALANCE 95

CHAPTER SEVEN 115

HOW TO ACHIEVE YOUR GOALS AND GET THE RESULTS YOU WANT 115

CHAPTER EIGHT: 134

HOW TO BREAK UNHEALTHY HABITS 134

CHAPTER NINE: 161

HOW TO IMPROVE ALL YOUR RELATIONSHIPS

.... 161

CHAPTER TEN 184

HOW TO BE A SUCCESS 184

CHAPTER ELEVEN 205

HOW TO TRULY BELIEVE IN YOURSELF 205

ACKNOWLEDGEMENTS 225

CLIENT Praise 227

FOR THE AUTHOR 227

INTRODUCTION:

This not just 'another life coaching book'. No, really, bear with me.

This is very, very different.

What makes this book essential reading - and different to other self-help manuals – is that it distils my own crazy life experiences alongside the coaching tools and techniques I have honed from working with thousands of clients over more than 15 years and delivering genuinely life-changing results. This book presents my personal story and my own unique way of working in a friendly, approachable, 'you-can-do-it' way. Because you can.

It is a practical guide that will help people to understand and address the specifics of their own thinking, which is the real key to realising how problems in life can become emotional blockages, and how to make the fundamental changes that will provide solid foundations for the future.

I focus on helping people to overcome the deep-seated limiting beliefs that hold them back from being the person they want to be; I help them to step out of emotional childhood and bring them into emotional adulthood, living the life they truly desire and deserve. I teach people how to stop blaming anyone else for how they feel and instead how to step into a strong, powerful, unshakeable mindset.

So, if you have a problem or two in your life, you are certainly not alone, and if you are reading this, you have picked up the right book. I will help you deal with any issues you may be struggling with, including relationships, self-esteem, anxiety, lack of confidence, as well as alcohol or body image/food obsessions. I can help you.

You will learn that before you can let a problem go or work your way through it, you need to understand the thoughts and beliefs that lie behind it. Thoughts create feelings, so starting to think carefully about your thoughts is key. Positive thoughts create positive feelings, which means negative thoughts create negative feelings! But this is not a 'positive thinking book', this is not about affirmations standing in a mirror repeating a sentence you don't believe.

No, this is a book teaching you the real-life, 'how-to'.

You may think that the problem you are facing is a very real thing; a concrete issue that surely anyone could see, but how 'real' it is depends entirely on the way that you are thinking about a particular situation. Remember, though, a thought or belief doesn't make something a fact.

In order to fix a problem, you need to fix your mind. And, by the way, I don't have a magic wand or the ability to 'fix' you (if anyone ever says that to you run a mile!). But what I can do is even more powerful than that: I can help you to get conscious and aware of the magnificent power of your mind and teach you the tools for how to think, in order to change your life - tools we never get taught at school.

Think of this book as a user-friendly manual for your mind.

**

CHAPTER ONE:

MY LIFE STORY

My battle with anorexia and drug addiction and how I turned my life around

FAMILY LIFE

In many ways, you could say I had a charmed childhood. I was brought up in a beautiful seven-bedroom house in North London, within walking distance of grandparents, aunts, uncles and cousins. I remember visiting my grandparents every Sunday with my parents and older sister for large, noisy family get-togethers. There would be lots of biscuits and home-made cake alongside plenty of laughter and chatting among the adults while the children would run around playing: us girls would take out my grandma's nail polishes when she wasn't looking and the boys would mess about with any electrical gadgets they could find. I felt the love and warmth of a close family, safe and secure in our leafy suburban oasis.

I adored my parents and was particularly close to my father, who was always in a good mood, laughing and joking and happy to spend time with me and my sister. He was a real superhero in my eyes, flying light aircraft for a hobby. Once, he put an old plane in the garden for us to play in, much to the dismay of my mother. I remember she was very annoyed and told him the only way the plane could stay was if she could plant lots of flowers to cover it! My father was a self-made successful businessman and my mother ran a fashion boutique until I was aged three when she sold it to become a full-time housewife and mum. Each morning, she would walk us to school, which was just up the road, and make us recite our times tables or learn our spelling lists along the way. Life couldn't have been more comfortable or carefree.

You know how you take on different roles in a family? My sister, who is two years older, always had a cheekiness to her; she was mischievous and pretty and popular. I took on the role of being the "good girl", so that no one had to worry about me. I remember thinking quite clearly from around the age of seven that this was my place in the family. My mum was very loving but always extremely busy; she would always have many pressing things to do. I didn't want to be a burden, so I worked hard at school, helped around the house and generally played the 'dutiful daughter'. I made sure to get good grades and my motto at that age was "whenever you need me, I'll be there."

My parents had always encouraged my sister and I to be independent; to think for ourselves and to work out our own problems or issues. Instead of just telling us what to do, they would offer us their opinion and then let us come to our own conclusions. You could say this was quite progressive parenting and a form of tough love that would hold us in good stead when we went out into the wider world.

But around the age of ten, my life changed. My parents started going abroad for long periods, leaving us in the care of nannies. One of the things they loved the most was spending time in the sunshine, so they would escape to Florida during the cold London winter months. They would ring every day to check in, but I suddenly felt very alone. I wasn't getting on with my sister – of course, I wanted to be part of her gang, but she wouldn't let me, as is usually the case with older siblings! – and with so much time to myself, I began to feel lost and insecure. Having been a confident, outgoing little girl, I began to withdraw into myself and started to sub-consciously associate love with being unavailable.

As a child, you learn behaviour that will shape you as an adult; you give meaning to something that might not necessarily be true, but it's how your young brain processes information and interprets situations. For me, with my parents absent for large chunks of time, I learnt that love was out of reach and began to associate it with a form of loss. I started to make assumptions that if I was worthy or of value as a person, then I wouldn't have been left behind. This was to have a huge impact on the kind of relationships I formed when I was older, which you can read more about in Chapter 9 on relationships.

I'll never forget the day that I first became aware of not feeling good about my appearance. It was my sister's birthday party and I was ten-years-old. I had never thought about how my body looked until I tried on a frilly denim skirt (it was the 1980s and I was all about the frills!) that belonged to her. We were in her bedroom with a group of her friends. The skirt clearly didn't fit me, but I kept trying to get it over my hips. My sister was tall and skinny – she was nicknamed the 'stick insect' in our house – but it had never crossed my mind to attach any meaning to that phrase as a little girl. I persisted with trying on the skirt, but could feel the looks and hear the quiet sniggering from the older girls in the room, and I remember thinking, "This isn't good".

For the first time in my life, I felt embarrassed and 'less than' and not good enough. I felt like I didn't 'fit in'. It was the moment my body issues started. That skirt had sown a seed of body dissatisfaction in my head because I truly thought: "If I was good enough, I would have fitted into it." No one had said to me, "You're not good enough", but that is the meaning I attached to the skirt incident.

BLACK EYES AND BULLYING

With my parents often away, I learnt to keep my feelings to myself. I didn't want to worry them. After all, I couldn't stop them going away and I'd been taught that independence was a good thing, so I just had to put a smile on my face and get on with it. But my teenage years were hell. I went to a small private girls' school and had the misfortune to end up in a particularly bitchy year group. At the time, I had no idea why I was singled out for bullying, but looking back, I imagine some of my classmates were seemingly envious of what they thought my life looked like from the outside.

I vividly remember one incident when I was about 13. All the girls used to hang out in the cloakroom and as I walked past, they shouted, "We hate Jacqueline Hurst!" It was an absolutely horrible, spine-chilling moment and something inside me broke then. I just thought, "Why? What did I do? Why would they say that? What is wrong with me?" I assumed it was my fault that no one liked me.

The resentment towards me at school turned into daily bullying. When one girl decided she didn't want to be my friend, the rest followed suit. They would either ignore me or hurl abuse at me, and before long, the verbal assaults became physical. I was pushed down the stairs and hit in the face. Yet, I still didn't say or do anything. I kept myself to myself to avoid my tormentors, spending every break time alone. I was too scared of reprisals to confide in my teachers, and with my parents usually away, I would retreat to my bedroom after school, feeling worthless and utterly alone.

I remember coming home one day, aged 15, and sitting at the top of the stairs nursing a black eye from being beaten up at school. My parents were in America and the nanny and my sister were in their rooms. The phone rang and it was my mum, who said: "Hi, darling! How are you?" I automatically gave my stock reply of, "I'm fine", concerned I'd disappoint her if I admitted I wasn't okay. Since she and my father valued independence in us so highly, I didn't want to let them down. I was so focused on putting other people's feelings ahead of my own and not being seen as weak, that I was prepared to silently endure both my emotional and physical pain. It was, as I was to learn later, classic co-dependent behaviour – putting a lower priority on my own needs while placing greater value on the approval of others. It wasn't until years later that I told my mum how I really felt and she was naturally devastated. I do not blame anyone for what happened, though, and we're now extremely close.

But at the time, as an impressionable, hormonal, lonely teenager, the situation was unbearable. Life was unbearable, and unsurprisingly, I began to look for comfort and approval elsewhere. I fell in with an older crowd outside school and discovered drugs. When one of the girls handed me a joint, I felt like I'd found heaven – the marijuana switched off all my feelings. I started smoking daily and also took up cigarettes and alcohol. For the first time in my life, I felt cool, like I was part of an 'in crowd', and I began to skip school and stay out all night.

Drugs became my life and my life became wild.

I discovered that if you're smoking dope, there's always someone who will want to join you. I was living the life of a 25-year-old at the age of 15 because I had complete freedom to do what I wanted; there was no one to reprimand me or look out for me. There was no one to answer to; no one to whom I had to justify myself or explain where I'd been.

On the surface, it was fun. During those crazy years, I went to fabulous parties, met a lot of famous people, including the artist Prince, and dined out at some of London's best restaurants. But it was all a façade.

Looking back, I was lucky to survive some of my more reckless escapades: on drug-fuelled nights out, I would sometimes end up in different countries on a whim – Spain, Italy, France, you name it. I once went to Spain with a man after losing a bet that I would win a game of backgammon against him. He turned out to be a very dangerous man and I literally had to make a run for it back to Britain. I was 20 at the time and so naïve.

MY ANOREXIC YEARS

It was no coincidence that I became seriously anorexic around the time my love affair with drugs started. With my life spiralling out of control – thanks to the constant bullying and drug-taking – my body (and what I ate) was the one thing I did have control over. Becoming skinny gave me something to aim for and to become 'good at' during what was essentially, a very confusing, unhappy time for me. Growing up in a weight-obsessed culture, being bombarded with supermodels in every glossy magazine, music video or advert, I thought that the thinner I was, the better I would be as a person. It wasn't even so much about how I looked; it was more about craving control. I was also struggling with turning into a woman; I didn't want the attention from boys, so I tried to make my body shrink.

I remember clearly the tipping point. I went on a diet (warning: diets don't work!) to lose weight before going on holiday to Spain with an older female friend, with whom I am still close. I actually said to myself, "I want to get thin". When we were there, we smoked loads of drugs and I felt amazing. It was the beginning of my ten-year battle with anorexia.

Drugs provided the perfect vehicle for keeping the weight off. In my unwell mind, I had reached the conclusion that using them was fine because they helped me to stay thin. From the age of 15 to 25, I was on a rollercoaster, veering between anorexia and bulimia, exercise addiction and starvation. I became extremely regimented about food, skipping meals and having a cappuccino or an apple only at specific times. But the more I tried to control my food intake, the less control I had. I never felt thin enough.

As my illness progressed, I became addicted to amphetamine diet pills and then cocaine. The disruption that caused around me was immense. My parents had no idea about the drugs and didn't know how to broach the subject of my anorexia. But I remember my father's worried looks, implying, "What are you doing to yourself?" Once, he blurted out: "Men prefer real women, Jacqueline" after being shocked by just how thin I was when he happened to see me emerging from the bathroom, wrapped in a small towel. Still, I insisted I was fine. I avoided family meal times by saying I was going to a friend's house (in reality, I was going to the gym to exercise obsessively) or pretending I'd already eaten and wasn't hungry. During one excruciating family meal, my sister exploded at me, saying, "You're not eating anything. This is ridiculous!" I managed to swallow a piece of broccoli before disappearing to my room. Every time, she tried to confront me about my disordered eating, I would go on the defensive and shut her out.

Later, I learned how upset she had been and that she had begged my mother to "deal with it". But my mum didn't know how to help. She told me later she was terrified that confronting the issue would make me worse. I do believe that nothing she could have said would have made any difference.

As you will read in more detail in Chapter 8 on breaking habits, I eventually became very sick. I had dizzy spells and fainted regularly. My hair began to fall out to the extent that I had bald patches at the back of my head and my fingernails stopped growing. I found it difficult to breathe and concentrate. At my lowest point, both mentally and physically when I tipped the scales at just 40kg and just before I finally reached out for help, the only clothes I could find to fit me were in the children's department – for a seven-year-old girl.

DRUG ADDICTION

At 16, I decided to leave school, even though I had been predicted straight As at A-level. I was desperate to get out into the 'real world'; to earn a living and travel to far away, exotic destinations. I most definitely didn't want to turn into the people I grew up around: married to my childhood sweetheart with two kids and a dog, and living next door to my parents. I wanted bigger, more exciting things.

When I was 17, I moved into a flat of my own with my parents' permission. I was showing the independence they so prized. But, of course, it also meant I could use drugs more easily. I became what is known as a functioning addict –

high most of the time and managing to complete a secretarial course (I can't remember any of my shorthand!) and hold down a succession of jobs. Somehow, I was able to work hard and do well – as PA to a retail director of a famous London store and then as PA to a lovely boss in a property company, among other jobs. As soon as I got home, though, I would take cocaine, which would sometimes keep me up all night. Occasionally, I would join friends in a club or try and go on an actual date, but most of the time, I was alone in my flat.

Increasingly, I cut myself off from my family and friends. Drugs became my best friend and my sole motivation to put one foot in front of the other. I still worked but only so I could afford to feed my secret habit. Drugs didn't reject me and were always available, and best of all, they helped to numb my feelings, masking the aching pain of loneliness and never fitting in.

Looking back, it must have been an incredibly distressing time for my family. They never knew exactly what was wrong with me because I hid it so well – I would wear super baggy clothes and a baseball cap to disguise how thin I was - but they could tell I wasn't right. On the few occasions I saw my parents, my worried mother would ask, "Are you bipolar? Are you depressed?" It's difficult now to recall how awful I was to them because today my family is my life. I was totally unreliable and uncommunicative, and at times, downright rude and ungrateful. I failed to turn up to key family events, such as my sister's birthday, and when I did go along my behaviour was erratic. Living in a twilight world of addiction, I felt as though they weren't 'my people' and didn't know or understand me.

The first time I tried to end it all, I was 20. I felt I had nothing left to live for and remember thinking, "I just can't take it anymore" and "I don't care what happens to me". It wasn't a conscious suicide attempt but one miserable day, I swallowed about 12 diet pills – the recommended dose was two – and lay on my bed petrified as the amphetamines coursed through my body and my heart raced out of control. I knew I had gone too far, though, and just hoped and prayed the sensation would pass. Somehow, possibly because my tolerance was so high, I managed to survive without needing to be hospitalised.

By the age of 25, I had absolutely hit rock bottom. By then, I'd walked out of my job, split up with my boyfriend at the time and was living in what was effectively a filthy squat. I was no longer speaking to my family and my life had become very small. That was the second time I tried to overdose. I remember sitting on my sofa one morning thinking it would be better for me to die, and taking a combination of drugs and alcohol. Again, miraculously, I survived.

RECOVERY & RE-LEARNING

Shortly after, my mother came to visit me completely out of the blue. I almost fell into her arms. She gave me a big hug and asked how I was. "Where has my beautiful daughter gone?" she said sadly. Something inside me clicked and I realised, in that moment, that all this had to stop. I had to stop. I finally saw how worried she was and that I no longer needed to pretend to her that I was okay. For the first time, I was able to admit I needed her help: "Mum, I am a drug addict."

This was to be the start of what was to be one of the toughest years of my life – getting clean. I knew I had to get better because the alternative was so bleak. My mother vowed to do whatever it took to help me, so I asked her to take me to a Narcotics Anonymous (NA) meeting. It was 27 August 2003 and I was 25 years old.

Mum was constantly there to support me, calling every day to make sure I'd eaten and been to my meetings. I remember turning up at the family home on one occasion, literally falling to my knees as she opened the door and sobbing to her, "I can't do it, I can't do it". She was amazing, telling me: "You *can* do it."

For a long time, it was all I could do to attend the meetings – three times a day in the beginning. I didn't participate at first because I had retreated so far into myself I'd forgotten how to speak! I did not know how to communicate without drugs and I couldn't even say my own name, let alone have a conversation with people. I went to every meeting in my over-sized clothes to disguise my painfully-thin frame, with my hoodie up and jaundiced eyes downcast.

I had to learn how to function in the real world again as I hadn't done anything without being either stoned or drunk for so many years. I had to learn how to have a shower, brush my teeth, pay a bill, have a normal conversation – all the basic human functions and activities we take for granted. They say when you do the 12-step programme that it can take up to three years to feel normal again, and that's so true. Getting clean was like thawing out; a minute-by-minute, hour-by-hour, day-by-day process.

Emotionally, it was even harder. I had to re-enter the troubled mindset of my 15-year-old self – the point at which my life froze – and learn how to feel again. Progressing through the 12 Steps, I had a lot of unlearning to do. I had a lot of resentment to let go of; a lot of apologies to make, and a lot of deep diving into allowing each feeling to come to the surface, to be able to process those feelings in the cold light of day and then learn to release them.

But as tough as my journey to recovery was, I knew there was no going back. I knew I wouldn't be able to "pay the bill emotionally" if I relapsed, in the sense that the price would be too high for my mental health. Somehow, I just had to keep putting one foot in front of the other.

But drugs and alcohol were only part of my recovery. Learning how to eat again was agonising and an even harder illness to deal with because you can stop taking drugs or drinking alcohol with a lot of courage, tenacity and effort, but you can't 'come off' food if you want to continue living. I'd also added an exercise addiction to my repertoire of afflictions, having taken up running in lieu of drugs, to try to find some sort of sanity in my life. At one stage, I was running about 100 miles a week, eventually causing my hip to collapse. I ended up having an operation that put me on my back for three months – but that's another story!

I had to accept that being thin didn't make me happy – it was not sustainable - and I knew that if I was going to get well, I would have to eat, but I was in a lot of emotional pain as I started to put on weight for the first time in years. My biggest fear was realised when I went from a size 00 to 16 as my body rebelled against all the years of starvation - and I ate and ate.

I talk more about my journey to overcome my eating disorders in Chapter 8, but, essentially, it was about learning to trust myself again. And doing the work on myself. Over the years, I saw countless therapists and attended various groups and centres, but they all seemed to tell me the same thing: that I needed a meal plan and should write down everything I ate each day. That was confusing to say the least, because it was still a form of control and control was the root of my problem. Meal plans are not the answer when you have an overwhelming fear of putting on weight. Being reminded of what you are consuming is not even remotely helpful. It simply made me want to control even more.

It was when I was at my heaviest that I had another breakdown – which, of course, eventually became another breakthrough - and decided I needed help. By chance, I came across a therapist in New York, who was to be my saviour in recovery and self-discovery. She taught me that I had to stop rebelling against my body and start rebelling instead against society. I had to surrender in order to accept and love myself and understand that the fight wasn't with myself but with the myth perpetuated by our diet-obsessed culture and the impossible goal of trying to attain perfection.

Hating your body is not a natural way to feel but there is a huge industry invested in brainwashing us to think that way as there would be a complete economic collapse if every woman around the world suddenly woke up tomorrow, stopped judging themselves and each other, and were totally happy with the way their bodies looked.

Once I made the fear-inducing decision to stop dieting once and for all and go into 'allowance', my body naturally balanced itself out from all the starvation, bingeing, restriction and dieting. It was as though it needed to recalibrate before it could stabilise again – ironically, back to my healthy, pre-diet weight when I was 15 before any of this started. My weight has been pretty much the same ever since – the irony of trying to control the uncontrollable is not lost on me nor sense of peace I've since achieved of being 'in acceptance'.

Today, I don't define my worth by the fact that my jeans might be a bit tight around my waist, my butt or my thighs from time to time. It doesn't matter. It's taken a long and winding road for me but I have finally stepped away from the persistent and insidious judgment that goes on around me - and around all of us. And let me tell you, that is a very liberating place to be.

Over the past 15 years, I've studied all over the world as my interest in self-development grew, and discovered self-help authors such as Dr Wayne Dyer, Eckhart Tolle, Marianne Williamson and Byron Katie. Learning about their ways of thinking helped me to change my own mindset. I realised my thoughts were the answer to my problems – and if I could get those right, I would get everything else right.

The U.S. is way ahead of the UK in the self-help field, so I started travelling there to take courses and to train in neuro-linguistic programming (NLP). I began my formal studies at the exclusive Bennett Stellar University in Miami and went on to train further in the 'Austin Method' of Advanced Structured Hypnotherapy in London and at the prestigious Life Coach School.

I began to feel that this was my calling in life, and in 2007, I became a full-time life coach, qualified hypnotherapist and NLP master practitioner. I also combine cognitive behavioural therapy with everything I've learnt over the years. As important as these formal qualifications are, I really believe that my life experience and intuition are key to my success. I define my approach as "helping people to step into emotional adulthood", so they can stop blaming others for how they feel and ultimately, be at peace with themselves.

I work with clients from all over the world who feel stuck, unable to change patterns of behaviour or move forward with issues and problems, including confidence, anxiety and stress and, of course, unhealthy habits and eating disorders.

I've also got an amazing relationship with my family now and speak to my parents and my sister every day. I have zero anger or resentment and feel nothing but love. Every single thing that happened, helped to get me to where I am today. I don't believe in regrets or in blaming others. I am not a victim.

In fact, what this journey has taught me is just how strong and resilient I am - and always have been. I just didn't realise it until I did the work and learnt to believe in myself.

What would I say to my 15-year-old self today? I would put my arms around her, tell her how much I love her and say, "You are amazing, you are strong and, although your journey will be different to most people's, you will get through the hard times and you will be okay."

Every day I feel grateful I'm still alive. These days I grab life with both hands and believe that anything is possible. I believe that we can do or be or have anything we want once we truly learn how to manage our minds. Each experience from my own story taught me so much. I am grateful for every single lesson and for being in a position now to give back and help others.

I hope this book, even in some small way, can help you, too.

CHAPTER TWO:

HOW TO GAIN CONTROL OVER YOUR THOUGHTS AND ACTIONS:

Do you find you have no control over your thoughts, feelings or behaviour?

It might be that you think you have no control over your thoughts or feelings or behaviour, which is extremely common and, in many ways, completely understandable.

The fact is, we are not taught *how* to think; how to process or understand our thoughts and beliefs. At school, we study many subjects – maths, geography, history, languages, religious education and PE. Of course, all of these subjects are important and relevant in terms of giving us a well-rounded education but they don't teach us the basics of how to manage our minds and, in turn, manage our feelings and behaviour. We're not taught at school how to think correctly for ourselves or how to act in our own best interests. If we learnt how to *really* think, then all of our lives would be very different.

No one says, "This is how you manage your mind", which is why so many of us get stuck – without even being aware of it.

In the absence of a conscious ability to think for ourselves, we rely, instead, on a learned belief system that can be faulty at best, and dangerous at worst. Often passed down from generation to generation, culturally-formed beliefs take root in the unconscious mind from a young age, and ultimately, control how we think, how we feel and how we behave. Harsh as it may sound, many of your beliefs will be entirely faulty – because they are wholly and solely a reflection of your past conditioning and experiences. The fact is that your current beliefs, while they may be extremely adept at giving you a negative or pessimistic perspective, are often irrelevant and possibly untrue.

They are based on a belief system, which in itself, is based on other people's views, opinions and beliefs about the world.

In other words, it is likely that you have been living your life with someone else's programming in your mind. As a baby you are essentially an 'open book', holding no opinions or making no judgments, until those involved in your upbringing – your 'tribe' - take it upon themselves to instil in you their own good opinions. Everything you know as an adult, you learnt from those early 'life' teachers, and it's normal that you should continue to hold most of what they taught you to be true, whether religious or cultural beliefs, political or societal views. Your teachers at school, your gender, your race, the society and culture you've been raised in, plus your religion, the friends you've made and even your ancestors, all have a part to play in shaping you and your opinions.

The question is, how often do we stop to think about what lies behind our opinions, though? How often do we reflect on what we were taught in our formative years and if those thoughts and beliefs are working for or against us today? How many of us have ever been taught that we can control what we think? And that is precisely my point!

If we're being truthful, we would most probably admit to ourselves that it is not often that we stop to question whether we want to keep this programming and continue to hold the beliefs we have been taught, or if we would actually prefer to change them. Challenging your programming is the first step in breaking free from any old, outdated beliefs that could be holding you back. Questioning them means you are giving yourself a choice as to what you want to believe.

ASK THE RIGHT QUESTIONS

The best way to challenge prior unquestioned programming is to start by asking the right questions. The questions you ask yourself are the key to self-development and growth. By asking yourself the right questions, you will start to focus your mind and challenge your thoughts, ultimately helping you to make the right changes, and in turn, achieve the right results. Conversely, asking yourself the wrong questions (which are ineffective, negative or just simply unhelpful), will only lead you to become confused and disheartened.

It is important, though, that the questions you ask yourself are powerful, honest and laser sharp if you want to make real progress. One of the most effective – yet simple – questions to always ask yourself is, "Why?". I can tell you, it will shake up your mind like never before!

As I will explain, our beliefs are basically thoughts that we choose to think over and over again – and which we have decided are true – often without question. We have thousands of thoughts coursing through our brain every day (approx. 60,000!), but only the ones that we *believe* to be true have any power. They are an automatic filter through which we experience our own subjective reality. But what if I told you that our beliefs are not facts; that our thoughts are not always facts, and that they are simply mental constructs you have created in your mind.

It is really important to learn the difference between facts and thoughts as this is exactly how we get ourselves into trouble. In order to differentiate, just remember:

- A thought is a construct in your mind
- A fact is something that is true and can be proved with evidence

For example, we all know that if we go to the supermarket on Saturday, that is a fact. However, if we say we feel "overwhelmed" going to the supermarket, then that is a thought. Each of us will have a different thought about the experience of going to the store.

If your beliefs are self-limiting, it's like you are walking through life with the wrong prescription in your glasses. Imagine for a minute if you were given the wrong lenses, your image of the world would be distorted and things would seem pretty negative. As a result, you would find obstacles at every turn, stumbling into them and harming yourself in the process because you can't *see* properly.

Thoughts generate feelings, feelings generate actions and actions generate your outcome – and negative thoughts always create negative feelings. If you continually say to yourself, "there's something wrong with me" or "I can't possibly get through this" or "I will never find the right job", then your thoughts are likely to be a self-fulfilling prophesy.

When you fill your mind with scary, limiting beliefs, it's not surprising that you will feel anxious or scared – you are quite literally using the power of your mind to make yourself feel awful. Through the negative use of your mind, you are fooling yourself into thinking there is a very real problem, when actually, it's all in your mind.

We seldom challenge our own beliefs head-on - in fact, we are actually inclined to seek out proof to confirm that our belief is true, especially if it happens to be a negative one. We keep finding more and more evidence for that reinforcing negative belief. We are hardwired to always seek out evidence to confirm our beliefs – however negative or destructive they may be. And as a result, we become habitually involved in negative thinking patterns, which, in turn, perpetuate negative feelings.

THE CHOICE IS YOURS

So, how do we change this mindset? How do we start to gain control over our thoughts and behaviours? Well, I'm here to tell you that you have that power now. YOU have the power to change your underlying negative beliefs by learning how to think correctly.

I am going to show you how to step away from damaging, hurtful and outdated beliefs and move towards empowering, strong and positive beliefs that will help you to achieve the life you love.

Let's jump into a quick worksheet.

Start by examining your most limiting or negative belief and asking yourself:

Where and when did I learn this belief?

_____

_____

What thoughts got me to this belief?

_____

_____

How long have I held it for?

_____

_____

How does it hold me back?

_____

_____

What would my life look like without this belief?

_____

_____

If my friend held this belief, what would I say to them?

_____

_____

Can I believe that for myself?

_____

_____

The main thing to understand is that you have the option to choose what you believe. We get a choice over what we think and believe, so changing our thoughts will change our feelings. Our mindset has to be right first, though, in order for our behaviour to change; in the same way popular culture urges us to cleanse our bodies with special detox diets, we also need to detox our minds. When people come to me with problems or negative feelings, one of the things I tell them is that even if they can't control the situation they're in, they can control the way they *think* about it. Being able to feel better in the moment and take control of your thoughts is the most useful thing you can do when trying to find happiness.

Of course, I'm not saying that it is easy to just switch a thought process but I want you to know that you can. It's all up to you and your thinking and when you learn to think consciously; when you become truly aware and opt to choose good-feeling thoughts, then you will be amazed at how your life will really change.

Throughout history, there are examples of famous people who have chosen to overcome past conditioning and experiences and embrace their own positive belief systems – ranging from aviation pioneers the Wright Brothers, whose flying machine invention was initially ridiculed, to Oprah Winfrey, who rose from poverty to become a billionaire philanthropist and arguably the world's best-known talk show host. It's hard to believe now that she was fired from her first broadcast job in America because she was unable to divorce her emotions from her stories and was deemed "unfit for TV"!

Most of the time when you find yourself struggling with something in your mind, it is when you are holding onto beliefs that are no longer true for you, which are negative and could be hindering you. Ask yourself, "What is my most limiting belief, my most negative belief, and where do I think that comes from?" Once you've identified that belief, find the evidence you are giving yourself to back it up and then start to seek evidence – that you already possess – to prove that this limiting belief is not true. This, in turn, will help you to start thinking differently and enable you to choose a new, more positive belief.

For instance, if you think you are the only person who is never going to meet a life partner, then you are likely to feel sad or defeatist from the get-go and probably won't make the effort needed to meet someone. I would challenge you to ask yourself instead: "How do I know that's true?" The answer is you don't – unless you happen to have a crystal ball! - so you need to examine that negative belief and how it is holding you back, and start to think more positively and optimistically. In doing so, you may open yourself up to the possibility of finally meeting someone.

Seek out evidence to disprove the negative and confirm the positive, instead. But please remember to practice self-compassion and go gently with yourself.

I once had a client who struggled with making friends and thought that no one liked him. He felt lonely, insecure and lacked self-confidence as a result. But not only was that belief negative, it was also clearly wrong. It was his inner critic – that inner dialogue we all have going on that will remain negative unless challenged and managed – that was convincing him he was not worthy of friendship. And because he thought it was hard to make friends, it proved to be the case. By realising he wasn't alone in holding those thoughts and by setting himself the goal of making just one friend, he was able to move forward with more confidence, strength and purpose.

The more you get your mind right the better you will feel and, in turn, the more constructive your actions will be.

TOUGH TIMES

We also tend not to recognise the opportunities of being in a dark place and this is one of the key ways I try to help people who come to see me. I'm a big believer in contrast: if you don't know what you don't like, then how can you know what you do like? It's important to remind people that being in a bad place is not a bad thing - it's only bad if you 'think' it's bad and don't do anything about it.

The dark times are part of our life journey and we are all bound to encounter some speed bumps along the way. The most important two points to remember are: you're not alone and only you hold the key for your own success. Remember, you're stronger than you think you are, so don't let the bad times dictate how you go through life. Instead, seize the opportunities they offer and grow from all of your experiences, good and bad.

Here's an example of how I was able to turn what was a deeply traumatic experience into a profoundly empowering one through the power of positive thinking.

About five years ago, I was violently mugged by a group of four men. It was late in the evening, around 10pm, and I was getting out of my car outside my home while on the phone to my mum. I was chatting and laughing with her and not paying much attention to my surroundings, as we've all been known to do. Suddenly, I felt someone grab me from behind and throw me to the ground, then a second attacker started to pull my scarf tightly around my neck, making it difficult for me to breath. I started to scream and fight back and I remember in my mind I was thinking, "I have not come this far, to die here." Luckily, some people drawn by the commotion, began shouting at the men to get off me, from the top of the road. Someone called the police, but before they arrived, the would-be muggers jumped into a waiting car and sped off. It seemed like an eternity but the whole incident lasted no more than five minutes.

For the first 24 hours after the attack, I was terrified. I couldn't leave the house or even go to the toilet on my own. But after the initial shock had worn off, I realised I didn't want to sit in terror for the rest of my life because of one unfortunate incident. As I began to explore my thoughts and feelings about the attack, I realised that the terror I felt didn't come from the assault itself, it came from the thoughts I had about what had happened to me. Therefore, I had to find a different way to process my thoughts about the attack.

In looking at the situation differently, I realised that:

- When people started shouting at the attackers, they didn't stay and fight, they ran off because they were scared and cowardly (they were not so big and strong after all!)

- They intended to mug me, except I didn't have anything on me for them to take, so their mugging efforts were pointless!

- And most importantly, my best and strongest thought was: I actually 'mugged' the muggers - because when I sat down to fill out some forms for the police, I reached into my handbag and pulled out two Rolex watches which were not mine! The thieves had previously stolen these watches and were wearing them when they mugged me. During the attack, they had come off and fallen into my bag, which, if you think about it, is quite funny. (And no, the police wouldn't let me keep them!)

We often view encounters or events in our lives way too personally. We think situations are about us, but they never are. That mugging had nothing to do with me; it wasn't about me at all and it certainly wasn't my fault. It was more about what had compelled those young men to attack a lone woman in the street: what was going on in their lives to drive them to such a desperate and violent act? It helped me to see how lucky I was compared to them, and, of course, that thought made me feel better. As I say, it is about the thinking!

GAIN CONTROL OF YOUR MIND

It all comes down to realising that you have a lot more control over your own life than you realise. This is not to be confused with trying to control others or external events. As much as it may be human nature to try to control everything, we have no control at all over what other people think, say or do – in the same way, we can't control life situations, such as the weather or a delayed flight. Worrying about things outside of our control is a waste of our time. A far better use of it is to focus on how to take control of our own lives – or any situation we may find ourselves in – through our thoughts.

When I suggest this to clients, though, their initial response will invariably be: "But I can't control my thoughts", to which I will respond: "If you don't, then who does?" I love posing that question because once we realise that only we can control OUR own thinking, we will be empowered and able to put it into practice. That is, of course, if you do really want to feel better!

The truth is, no one can control your thoughts except you.

And remember, thoughts are what generate actions, which is why it is so important to make sure we are conscious of our thoughts because we can then start to take the actions that are right for us. The challenge is to remind yourself that you cannot control anything or anyone outside of yourself - start to monitor what's inside your head, instead.

Learning how to think differently is what is going to change your life. A different mindset will enable you to make better decisions – and for the right reasons. It's very easy to say, "I want to go to the gym", for example, but if you haven't put any real thought behind that decision or, in reality, consider it to be more of a chore than something you're excited about, then your fitness kick is bound to fail. Finding four or five strong thoughts that you believe to be true about going to the gym is what is going to help you turn your dreams and goals into reality.

This book will simply ask you to start to become conscious and aware. By this, I mean, start to become aware of your thought processes and how you actually use your mind to think. It's important to start here because nothing can be changed without awareness. You cannot change your thinking without being aware of what you are thinking in the first place!

Changing your life by changing your thinking is 100% possible. I have worked with more than 7000 clients over the past 15 years and the majority of them have told me, "this work has changed my life". Naturally, anything good that is worth having will take time, effort and patience, so you have to be willing to put in the work. Waking up your brain and becoming conscious won't happen overnight but it will happen, so be fearless!

The key is to change the way you think.

You need to power your thoughts with positivity – and from that, a sense of commitment and purpose will follow. It's about consciousness and waking up your brain, which is the most powerful tool in your body.

CASE STUDY

I once had the pleasure of helping a very lovely client who came to see me because she was struggling to have a baby. She wanted so much to be a mother but wasn't having any luck. When she turned up at my office for our first session she was very upset as she just couldn't get pregnant. She had tried naturally, she had tried with IVF and nothing was working. She was exhausted, down on herself and in a cycle of constant pain.. The first thing we did was to look at her thoughts in depth. She had a lot of limiting beliefs about getting pregnant so we worked together on her thinking around those beliefs. It's important to remember, we cannot control the situation, we can only control our mind. Her thoughts were along the lines of, "I don't think it is ever going to happen for me"; "I think there must be something wrong with me", and "it is so unfair that this won't happen". Over time, she was able to learn how to manage her mind and correct her belief system. She learnt that the more she stayed in the negative the worse she felt, and the more negatively she acted or behaved, the less she was likely to achieve the desired outcome of becoming a mum. When she understood it wasn't the situation that was creating her unhappiness, she was willing to delve into her thinking and change it. And the happier she allowed herself to be, the calmer she became and the more she radiated health and wellbeing. She worked hard at getting her thoughts right and in the middle of the first national lockdown I got this email from her:

"Jacqueline, I wanted to drop you a line to let you know how our baby journey ended. After I stopped seeing you, we went through a second miscarriage at 10 weeks, but after the next [embryo] transfer, by some miracle two of them stuck. Our gorgeous (biased!) twins were born in July and everyone is well and healthy. I am absolutely loving being a mum and my partner is a natural dad. I just wanted to say a huge thank you for your part in our success. You were fundamental in very quickly shifting how I thought about our struggle and enabling me to keep going through all of the toughness. You are amazing!"

Admittedly, I shed a little tear but I am very sure that without her changing her thinking, she would not be where she is today. Mental toughness, mental resilience, mental clarity – these are everything.

WORKSHEET

Write down some of the key thoughts that are running through your head for at least a week. Write down 5 a day for a week.

_____

_____

_____

_____

Look at the thoughts and see how they make you feel: Happy, sad, angry, hurt, indifferent, etc.

Next, see if you can reframe these thoughts – you can start to seek evidence to prove the negative might not be true.

Ask yourself, how would my life look without those negative thoughts?

_____

_____

_____

_____

It's funny how you can always manage to find positive evidence to disprove a negative thought by simply changing your perspective. For example, if you have a limiting belief that you will never have a partner in your life, challenge that belief:

How do you 'know' you won't?

_____

_____

Do you know the future?

_____

_____

Did you ever have a partner before?

_____

_____

Why would you be the only person on the planet 'not able to' meet someone? Etc. etc.

_____

_____

When you find yourself becoming properly conscious of your thoughts, then you will know you are on your way to making the changes you need.

CHAPTER THREE

HOW TO BEAT ANXIETY

Do you feel anxious and don't know how to stop feeling like that?

It's no surprise to learn that the number of people experiencing high levels of anxiety rose sharply during the Covid-19 pandemic – the equivalent of around 19 million adults in Britain – according to the Office for National Statistics. Parents, in particular, reported being in a state of constant red alert, worrying about the health and safety of elderly relatives; home schooling children while WFH, and holding onto their jobs – all against the backdrop of global uncertainty and fear.

Given that anxiety is defined as experiencing nervousness, unease or worry, typically about an event or something with an uncertain outcome, then it's completely understandable that many of us may have felt more anxious or stressed than usual.

What's important to know is that we all feel anxious from time to time; anxious about performing well at a meeting, hitting our targets at work, socialising or even going on a date. Anxiety can cause considerable disruption and distress to everyday life.

If you suffer from feeling anxious your symptoms may include nervousness, racing heartbeat, clammy hands, shortness of breath and a constant feeling that "something bad is going to happen". Other side effects range from fatigue and irritability to disturbances in sleep or eating habits. All these symptoms can seem overwhelming and may prevent you from enjoying a fully functioning daily life.

But the reality is - and I want you to keep your mind open - you CAN take back control and be free from anxiety. It is absolutely possible. This is because anxiety is simply a feeling created by a thought. Anxiety is totally possible to overcome with the right thinking. It sounds easy but I promise you it is true.

When you start to become aware of the thoughts you are choosing that are creating the anxiety, you then have an opportunity to be able to challenge and change those thoughts so that you are able to channel more positive and constructive thoughts which create more positive and constructive feelings!

What I want to stress is that most of the time, we *can* control our responses because anxiety is all in our heads. Often, it's caused by trying to project unhelpfully into the future and/or catastrophising about things that may or may not happen. Take the global pandemic, for instance. None of us knew what was going to happen, so there was no point trying to second guess the outcome. But we could control our thoughts about the situation and, therefore, how we handled it.

Rather than exist in a state of perpetual anxiety about whether you are going to lose your job or worry about a specific crisis you 'think' you might be facing, focus instead on the here and now - be thankful for the roof over your head and the health of your family, and see unforeseen challenges as an opportunity to do something new with your life - perhaps moving to the countryside or finally realising your dream to start your own business. Obstacles always lead to opportunities.

ANXIETY IS NOT AN EXTRA LIMB

When clients come to me with anxiety, they talk about it as though it's a physical part of them, like an arm or a leg. They view anxiety as a permanent fixture in their lives. They say they *have* anxiety, but while we are all born with arms and legs, we don't emerge into the world in a state of anxiety. It is a feeling or condition that we create through our thoughts.

We choose to feel anxious, which means it is completely within our control to change how we feel. Those who believe it is not possible to change how they feel, simply haven't learned how to manage their mind correctly.

Even at its most extreme, reducing anxiety is within your control. Many of us have experienced panic attacks at some point in our lives. This is when your body experiences a rush of intense physical and mental symptoms like shaking, palpitations, faintness, nausea, sweating, shortness of breath and hot flushes. Your mind is so powerful, it literally sets off a roller coaster of hormones in your own body. Pumping out hormones like adrenaline, norepinephrine and cortisol is your body activating the evolutionary 'fight, flight or freeze' response to perceived danger. But where early man needed that empowering rush of adrenaline to escape from life-threatening situations, these days we are more likely to go into 'fight or flight' mode in response to negative comments. How crazy does that sound – but it's true! The pre-frontal cortex in our brains (the part that involves critical-thinking, problem-solving and decision-making) becomes temporarily incapacitated as the focus turns to survival - and fighting or fleeing the so-called 'threat' of someone else's negativity.

However, once you understand that other people's words can't physically hurt you, you're in a stronger position to deal with those weird physical symptoms. Remember, it's just your hormones going into overdrive and you can control them by calming down your mind. The best way to do this is by concentrating (using your mind!) on slowing down your breathing. Make a point of watching your stomach rise up and down as you breathe into it for five minutes, up to three times a day. You'll be pleasantly surprised by how quickly your breathing will return to normal and how fast those scary symptoms disappear. Then you can start to tackle your thinking.

Another piece of advice I give to people when they come to me in a state of anxiety, is to write it out. Now this may sound a little strange but trust me, it's a very effective way of dealing with such feelings. I always suggest keeping a notepad and pen at hand so you can record whenever you get into a negative or anxious headspace. If a notebook isn't your style, you can use the memo app on your smart phone and write your thoughts down there. The main point is to recognise when you are feeling low, and by recording your thoughts, you will eventually become aware and conscious of your negativity. As I always say, feelings are just that – feelings. They cannot hurt or harm you – unless you choose to dwell in the negative. One of the biggest problems is when people don't even recognise what makes them upset; they just get caught up in the emotions and give in to the negativity. Writing down what thoughts you have which are negative and when they occur can help you get on top of controlling your mind. Being able to recognise when and what gets you down can help you better understand how to avoid slipping into that way of thinking.

If you find you're becoming obsessed with a thought that creates worry and anxiety, it's really important to retreat and retract. In other words, take a moment to chill it out. Take yourself out of your office or your home and go for a short walk, grab a coffee and just retreat. Then take a moment to stop, breathe and calm yourself down by reminding yourself that it is your choice to feel this way and that it may not the best choice for getting through the rest of the day.

STOP WORRYING ABOUT WHAT OTHERS THINK!

There's no doubt that anxiety can seem very isolating when you believe you're alone in what you're going through and that you are the only one in the world who feels like this. In these situations, try to open up to friends and loved ones about your thoughts and feelings as talking about things can help you to feel better right away and enable you to see things from a clearer and more realistic perspective. Just remember this: Anxiety is a choice. Choose a different thought and get a different feeling. For example, choose to feel 'calm' instead of 'anxious' and then ask yourself, "How can I think about this in order to feel calmer?". Remember, take it slowly and be gentle with yourself, but don't sit there thinking, "I can't do this". You definitely can because you are more powerful than you realise!

Of course, anxiety comes in many forms. So many of us are people pleasers and worry about what other people think of us; whether they like us or not. Many of us are programmed from a young age to crave approval from those around us and society at large – we have been taught by society to care what other people think but how many of us have questioned this belief? We are not mind readers – we do not know what someone else is thinking. If we did, we would all be making a fortune! None of us can read minds or do anyone else's thinking for them, so unless someone is totally straight with you about what they're thinking or feeling, then don't assume to know.

The key here is to not worry about what other people think. Firstly, because you can't control their thoughts and secondly, you can't make people like you. Clients will often say to me, "I've tried to be extra nice to my friend or colleague, so why don't they like me?" But the problem with trying to people please and going out of your way to seek approval or endorsement from others, is that you are not being authentic or true to yourself. One of the fundamental things I was taught when I was in recovery from my drug addiction back in the day, is that what other people think of me is none of my business. I learned through my own journey of self-development that we are here for bigger and far more important things and worrying about controlling what other people think, is not one of them.

One of my biggest lessons was understanding that if I spend time trying to control how someone thinks about me, I am not being genuine. I am all about truth and honesty, so not being authentic is not the game I want to play in life. Letting go of what others might think was one of the best things I learnt early on in my recovery.

I also learnt that not everyone is always thinking about ME! So many of my clients worry about what other people think but most of the time, other people are actually thinking about themselves, not you. It comes as a relief when you actually stop taking everything so personally.

In order to stop worrying about what other people think of us, we need to spend more time on learning to like – and love - ourselves. How can we ask other people to like us if we don't like ourselves? And if we're unhappy with ourselves, how can we truly love others?

Often our concerns about what other people think come from a place of deep insecurity. In an age of social media saturation, feelings of insecurity have never been more prevalent as we measure ourselves against others on a daily basis, striving for an idea of perfection that doesn't really exist.

The more insecure you are, the more anxious you are likely to be about what other people think. But remember, you can't assume to know what someone else is thinking so try to keep an open mind and take a different perspective. Ideally, choose to start thinking about what YOU are thinking, not what someone else is. This is how we grow.

For example, if your boss expresses disappointment in the company sales figures, you might automatically assume he's blaming you and start to feel under threat. If you adjust your thinking and understand that he's answerable to shareholders and investors and is probably under pressure himself, then you'll realise his response is not directed at you personally. Alternatively, you might blame your boss for not giving you certain opportunities or overlooking you for a promotion. Instead of wasting time on negative, defeatist thoughts, think about what you would like to achieve at work and how you can make that happen.

Likewise, if you go to a party and see someone there who you are convinced does not like you, then try to consciously change tack: rather than assume it's the other person who is causing the problem and that their behaviour or attitude is responsible for the way you feel about yourself, understand that it's coming from your own mind.

As the American tycoon Warren Buffet once wisely said: "You will continue to suffer if you have an emotional reaction to everything that is said to you. True power is sitting back and observing things with logic. True power is restraint. If words control you that means everyone else can control you. Breathe and allow things to pass."

Only you can take that powerful step of challenging – and controlling – your own thoughts. By practising a thought that feels better, you will eventually start to feel stronger and better about yourself. You'll be able to ask yourself, "Does it really matter if this person chooses not to like me?", and ultimately realise that even if they don't, you haven't lost anything.

Alternatively, you may surprise yourself and go on to establish a solid friendship. By getting rid of your preconceptions, you will be more open to understanding the other person's perspective on life and able to forge a deeper connection. Your insecurities will also begin to disappear. Another powerful question to ask yourself is: "Do I actually like this person and want to be their friend?" You may just as easily decide you do not. My dad once gave me a great piece of advice before a job interview: "It's not a matter of whether they like you, it's whether or not you think the job is right for you."

BE ACCOUNTABLE – TO YOURSELF

The only person you need to hold yourself accountable to is you.

I once had a client who came to me because she felt really insecure most of the time - even at what should have been such a lovely time, the run-up to her wedding. No matter what she did, she always felt like she just wasn't strong or confident enough in herself. It was really affecting her day-to-day life on both a personal and professional level, so we worked on her thinking until we discovered the thought that was creating a lot of her insecurity, namely, that she "didn't want to upset people". She kept doing things simply to please others, like keeping people in her life she didn't even like, for fear of upsetting them. She worked hard on changing her thinking and at the end of our time together sent me this email: "Hi Jacqueline, I did the most adult thing I've ever done yesterday and said goodbye to 'that' negative friend. I told her I only wished her well but she could never really seem to wish me well, and I couldn't look forward to an engagement party or wedding with that level negativity and paranoia from a 'friend'. As someone who is great at sending my feelings in a text - doing this over the phone was hard. But she has been the only person with anything negative to say about my engagement, so I did what I have not been able to ever do before working with you – and said goodbye to something that wasn't bringing me joy. Everything feels just more positive! Thank you again for working with me to learn the tools that have helped me become my best self."

Here's another example of how we create anxiety for ourselves. One of the most common side effects of giving up smoking is anxiety. But the reality is that nicotine disappears from your blood stream within one to three days, so there is no actual physical reason why stopping the habit should make you anxious. Of course, the feeling of anxiety is driven by an automatic assumption that quitting will be difficult. No one is saying it will be easy but if you try to see it as a positive act and a chance to do something that will have long-term health benefits, then you will find your mindset shifting – instead of getting to day four and feeling overwhelmed, consciously acknowledge how much progress you're making and start to feel empowered by that. In other words when you think differently, you feel better.

We have to train our minds to be strong, so we can do the things that are true for us, but that means putting in the work, requiring willpower, determination and plenty of practice. In the same way you might lift either a 2kg or 20kg weight at the gym, it's up to you to decide how strong you want to be mentally. The choice is yours. There is no magic bullet. You can choose to get fit – mentally and physically - or stay as you are. When someone says to me, "I can't do that", my response invariably is: "Well, prove it to me then?" You see, how do you know you can't do something if you're not willing to even try? Remember, though, this is not an overnight process; it will take time to fully change how you think, which is why consistency is important.

A lot of the time, we slip into default mode in terms of how we react to something or someone. We rely on our subconscious to guide us - but this is unconscious thinking and only serves to reinforce our own limitations. If you are constantly telling yourself phrases like "I always do X" or "I can't do Y", then you are quite literally instructing your brain to believe them to be true. As humans, we really do believe that what we think is always a fact. But when we believe that every thought we have is true, then we open ourselves up to a whole world of pain and stress. If a thought comes into your mind that "I'm not good enough" and you believe it, it can trigger a tonne of other negative thoughts and feelings. However, this is an un-managed mind. We have to learn to become mindful and recognise that our thoughts are not facts. You can do this by consciously asking your brain a series of questions, rather than telling it to accept statements as facts. If you opt for positive words over negative, your mind will process the information differently and the outcome is more likely to change for the better.

Be gentle with yourself. It's not a race. Start by making small adjustments. One client became terrified of going outside after being violently mugged, so I gave her a series of achievable goals to build her confidence and reduce her anxiety. She started by going to her front door and opening it, then progressed to short walks to the end of her street and back, and finally, one day, she turned up at my office with a bunch of flowers. She gradually took control over her fears and realised that the only thing stopping her from leaving the house was her own mindset.

Of course, we can't be positive and upbeat all the time and I'm not here to tell you that your feelings are wrong. Sometimes you need to stay in a feeling to be able to process it. For example, if you are grieving the loss of a loved one, it would be unrealistic and wholly inappropriate for me to say you shouldn't have that feeling. Only you can decide when the time is right to move forward; ultimately, it's your choice.

Personally, I know from bitter experience that it's not good for me to dwell on feeling negative. When my husband ended our marriage suddenly and without warning via a WhatsApp message, I was naturally devastated. I learned later that he had only married me because he wanted to get to the next level of seniority in the company he worked for and he had to be seen to be married, in order to be given the promotion. Unbelievable I know, but that was the case. Getting my mind – and thoughts - around what had happened took time. Gradually, I realised that he was, in fact, giving me an unexpected gift. Instead of viewing the end of my marriage as a huge loss, I was eventually able to feel relief that I'd had a lucky escape. Why would I want to be married to someone who treated me like that? It took time to reach this point but I knew I didn't want to remain forever in a state of negativity or anxiety, beating myself up about what had happened.

It's important not to judge yourself harshly.

For example, if you are prone to binge eating, stop to consider why you have suddenly inhaled that box of chocolate brownies. Our behaviour can serve as an alarm bell to make us examine our thoughts: Why am I feeling stressed or anxious? What are the lessons I can learn from these feelings? How can I change my thoughts?

Similarly, avoid making life-changing decisions until you have really taken the time to think about why you're intent on taking a certain course of action. Be honest with yourself. When a client comes into my office insisting they want to leave their partner, I tell them not to do anything until they have properly analysed their thoughts. A lot of it comes down to communication. Once a couple is willing to put in the effort to start talking through their problems, they will often begin to see things differently. It's not uncommon for clients to change their minds because once they change their mindset about the relationship, they find that – surprise, surprise - their partner does, too, and all that stress and anxiety caused by agonising over it seems to melt away.

CASE STUDY

One memorable client was a Russian tycoon, who swept into my office for his first session determined not to address what was making him angry - and was therefore in a permanent state of anxiety. When I told him that his homework was to stay angry, he became even more annoyed and literally stormed out. Although he was a big guy and physically intimidating, I wasn't in the least bit worried. I didn't care what he thought of me; I was there to do a job and it was up to him to decide whether he wanted to work with me or not.

Funnily enough, he sent me flowers a short time afterwards, apologising for his behaviour and asking to come to my office again. Not only was he accustomed to being in a position of power and control, he wasn't used to being challenged. But he quickly understood when I gave him the task of 'staying angry' as his homework, that he didn't actually want to be in that state all the time, and was finally ready to learn how to let the anger go and think differently, so he could feel better. It worked like magic!

WORKSHEET

Write down the thoughts that make you feel anxious or worried on a notepad.

_____

_____

_____

_____

_____

_____

Then imagine your friend is telling you this is how she feels.

For example, if the thought is: "I am freaking out about going out on this date later; what if it is just awful?", you could respond to your 'friend', saying: "But this is only dinner with a boy! He could be a really interesting person and you might end up having an enjoyable evening whether there is romance there or not. He might even be more scared than you."

By following through on your thoughts, you will make them seem less scary.

How would you answer her back?

CHAPTER FOUR:

HOW TO STOP FEELING STUCK

Do you feel stuck in a rut and want to get out of it?

How many times have you thought to yourself, "I just feel stuck"? It is one of the most common things people say when they come to see me. And yet, it is one of the most ill-defined.

Clearly, there's a problem but what does 'feeling stuck' actually mean? It is such a general expression, one that can encompass a whole range of negative feelings, including hopelessness, self-doubt, boredom, frustration and depression, that first you must identify exactly what it is that is making you feel stuck.

I want you to think for a moment if you have ever asked yourself any of the following questions: Why do you feel stuck? Where are you stuck? In what way are you stuck? What are you afraid of? You need to drill down through the generalities and work out precisely what the issue is. It won't be your entire life which is stuck; it will be one specific part of it, such as your job or your relationship.

So, the first thing is to be really clear about that. Question yourself as to what you are thinking that is making you feel the way you do, to enable you to get a specific fix on the problem. It all starts with the mindset, of course. If you are trapped in a negative thought process, then you will naturally create thoughts that zap your confidence and perpetuate uncertainty, doubt and fear.

Being stuck is an action - well, an inaction. When you are stuck, you are paralysed. You lack direction. You feel incapable of taking the action required to propel yourself forward and make the changes you instinctively crave. So first, look at how to stop yourself being paralysed.

In order to become un-stuck, you need to change your thinking. You need to change those negative thoughts to ones that create feelings of confidence, happiness and excitement. Once you can generate the right feelings, these will drive you to act.

So how are you going to create these feelings that will help you to move forward and stop you from being stuck?

Analyse what it is that you are thinking that is preventing you from taking those steps. Don't just say to yourself, "It's too difficult" or "I can't". You need to be more honest with yourself and very specific.

What actions do you need to take in order to make progress and become unstuck? Start by devising a plan for how to move from the situation you are in to the situation you want to be in. Write down what you are thinking and why those thoughts are not letting you act. Then, reframe your thoughts in order to feel better and take the action.

Don't allow negative thoughts to get in the way; just make a purely practical, hypothetical list of the steps that you would need to take to move from one situation to another. Do you need to research the requirements for a new career path? Do you need to take a training course of some sort? Is there someone you could talk to for advice? This is what will eventually enable you to become unstuck.

KICK-START YOUR MOTIVATION

Breaking things down into smaller, manageable chunks also helps. For instance, if you set yourself an ambitious goal of exercising for four hours each day, you are probably going to feel overwhelmed and end up doing nothing. But if you start by committing to just ten minutes daily, then you are more likely to feel inclined to take up the challenge. You need to kick-start your motivation; remind yourself that you are in control and only you have the ability to change your thoughts about the situation. How good do you feel once you've done those ten minutes of exercise? I thought so! That instant adrenalin rush, followed by feelings of empowerment and excitement, are proof that you are capable of change.

The first step is always the hardest but you will quickly find that this one activity will lead to other, more dynamic steps that will ultimately allow you to break free and live more intentionally.

Another helpful tip is to project into the future and look at where you want to be in five, ten or even 15 years' time. What do you need to do today in order to make that vision a reality? Our society is so geared towards instant gratification that we sometimes forget that it takes time, effort and perseverance to reach our goals.

All of this sounds relatively easy to achieve, so why do so many of us continue to stay 'stuck'? It's simple, really. Often, we choose to remain stuck because it's a convenient excuse not to shift out of our comfort zone. We may remain in our comfort zone because we think it is a comfortable and safe space - but it isn't at all! It's quite the opposite, in fact, because it keeps us small and makes us fearful of change; it fills us with doubt and uncertainty, and ultimately, regret, when we realise just how disappointed we are with our lives.

There's a popular saying: "a comfort zone is a beautiful place but nothing ever grows there", which sums up the paradox of being in that particular state. We are going nowhere when we are in our comfort zone. And we need to exit it fast, if we want to grow.

In the same way, we make wrong decisions in life because we hold on to thoughts and feelings that we think keep us safe but are often, in fact, holding us back.

We might even enjoy being stuck when we know that our situation, however unfulfilling, offers us financial and emotional security. For example, we might make excuses like needing to pay the mortgage or the school fees for staying in a dead-end job. Or we might put up with a dull and empty marriage because we convince ourselves that it's preferable to being on our own – after all, "better the devil you know".

We all have our set daily routines, whether eating meals at a certain time, visiting the same places or carrying out the same work tasks every day, which we convince ourselves are essential for living an orderly life. These daily activities can often become so mindless and mundane that we end up living on autopilot and feeling stuck as a result.

Yet, we rationalise this limiting approach to life by thinking it's less painful to sit in a familiar space than it is to make the effort required to open ourselves up to the inherent risk that new challenges and horizons may represent.

As celebrated American writer Richard Bach (of Jonathan Livingston Seagull fame) wrote in his best-selling book Illusions: The Adventures of a Reluctant Messiah: "Argue for your limitations, and sure enough, they're yours."

I absolutely love this quote. What it means is that instead of looking at the possibilities, you choose, instead, to look at every single reason why something can't happen. By limiting yourself, you are reinforcing your own incorrect beliefs that you are 'less than' and don't deserve success or happiness.

What you are doing, in fact, is making excuses for staying stuck. If you constantly come up with a million reasons as to why you can't find a solution to a particular problem or situation that is clearly holding you back, then you are most likely casting yourself as a victim. Excuses can range from blaming external forces such as the economy or your employer to your age, childhood trauma, illness or just plain bad luck.

As Albert Einstein memorably said: "You cannot solve a problem with the same mind that created it." You have to change your mindset if you are going to be able to shrug off that victim mentality.

This doesn't mean that whatever trauma you have suffered is diminished in any way and should be forgotten or pushed to one side if you are to overcome your victim status. All I'm saying is that if you continue to take a "poor me" approach to life, then you're unlikely to ever find happiness or fulfilment. You are going to stay stuck in an uncomfortable place that leaves you feeling powerless and helpless.

Take brothers Rob and Paul Forkan, who suffered unimaginable trauma after they were orphaned as teenagers when their parents Kevin and Sandra died during the Boxing Day tsunami of 2004. The brothers survived by clinging on to the roof of a building when the giant wave hit the Sri Lankan coastline, killing more than 280,000 people.

In 2012, they started selling flip-flops from their Brixton flat as a way of helping others and now run multinational clothing and accessories brand Gandys. Through the sale of their products, which are stocked in hundreds of stores, Rob and Paul, now both in their early 30s, fund Gandys Foundation, which works to build campuses and provide education for disadvantaged children in underdeveloped nations, including Sri Lanka, Malawi, Nepal and Brazil.

Revealing why he and his brother felt compelled to set up their foundation, Paul told MailOnline (22/05/2020): "What we went through was horrible but what we had seen as children travelling around the world was much worse in some ways. Other children don't have the support and care in place that we did."

Explained Rob in an interview with the Independent (27/05/2013): "We're trying to create something positive out of a negative. Our parents believed in the idea that if you fall off your bike, you get back on it. There's no point in feeling sorry for yourself and doing nothing with your life."

POSITIVE MINDSET

While the Forkan brothers' experience was undoubtedly extreme, everyone goes through rough times: whether it's a bad breakup, losing your job or saying goodbye to a beloved pet, negative times are just a part of life. What's important though is that you don't let those negative experiences define you. Instead of complaining about their misfortune or seeing themselves as victims, Rob and Paul were able to view their experience through the prism of a positive-thinking mindset and were inspired to achieve something incredible as a result.

I understand from some of my own traumatic experiences just how hard it can be to get over difficult situations. But every negative experience I've had in my life has always opened up a door to something new and better – like building my life coaching business and helping other sufferers after going through my own battles with drugs, alcohol and anorexia. I realise how easily our minds can go to negative spaces in the moment, but try not to waste valuable time and energy focusing on the past, when you could be spending that time building a better future for yourself. Obsessing over what went wrong is one of the worst things you can do for your mental health. Things might be tough now but deep down you are stronger than you can even imagine, so let go of those negative thoughts, take the lessons you have learnt from the experience and stride forward with confidence.

I really do believe that when one door closes another one opens, and if you are too busy trying to look behind the door that has closed you are not going to be able to jump through the bright new door that is about to open. From breakups to job loss, those things were meant to be; it's just how the universe works sometimes. It's okay to feel sad and yet how sad you want to stay, is totally your choice.

CHOICES

You see, it's all about choices. You always, always have a choice as to how you think, feel, act and behave. If you choose to maintain a destructive relationship or hold on to a demoralising job, then that's your decision. But if you stop blaming everyone else for where you are in your life or how you feel, and take responsibility, you will be able to grow into emotional adulthood. Growing into emotional adulthood will usually involve learning lessons from your past and making different choices. It requires you to be brave and to look inwards and properly scrutinise your thoughts. Ultimately, the only one who has any real responsibility for you and where you find yourself in life, is you.

Part of being open to changing our thoughts is a willingness to accept that we are worthy just as we are. Yes, read this again. You are enough. Right here, as you read this. You. Are. Enough. You may feel like you don't deserve to be happy, that you aren't good enough. But you need to cut yourself some slack and be prepared to forgive yourself. Being kind to ourselves is a fast track to helping us to let go. Choose a mentor - either someone you know or admire from afar - who is naturally assertive, knows how to set boundaries and has a strong sense of self, and learn from them. They will help you to become the best version of yourself possible.

As American entrepreneur and author Jim Rohn says, "You are the average of the five people you spend the most time with."

If you surround yourself with people who discourage rather than encourage you, it stands to reason that you are going to feel less inclined to pursue your dreams.

What's interesting is that when we say we feel 'stuck', we are acknowledging that we are aware that our thoughts are off-key and that we know that there is more to life. We might find ourselves saying things like, 'My life would be better if…'", and we forget that these are the choices we made for ourselves. But if we don't like the choices we have made, remember, we can always change our minds.

Our gut feelings are very real, and when we're not living in our truth, our inner self knows this. We just need to listen to ourselves more.

Very often, what is making people feel stuck and frustrated is that they know there is something bigger for them which their life is not offering at the moment, and they are 'stuck' with the fact that they are not living this better life which they would prefer.

Say you are a lawyer but want to be a fashion designer. How do you begin to address this? Just wanting a huge change is too general. What are you thinking about the issue which is making you feel stuck? Are you thinking that you can't do this sort of thing? Are you saying to yourself that you would never be able to be a designer? Don't say these things to yourself, because none of them are true, it is just what your mind is saying to you.

Let your imagination move forward. How would you feel if you had already achieved the outcome that you so desire? Let's say you have created and shown your first fashion collection and received rave reviews. How amazing and wonderful would that feel? How brilliant and powerful and unstoppable would that be? Revel in that feeling and hang onto it to help you take the first practical steps towards becoming unstuck and realising your plan.

REALISE YOUR POTENTIAL

It's very common for people to feel trapped in their jobs. When people tell me that they that they can't leave the job they hate because they need the money, I usually say you don't have to leave right now. Being responsible, paying your bills and taking care of your loved ones are all hugely important, but there is always room to reach higher. You may not have the means to leave your job right now, but you can begin preparing for that jump. Do some research and see what opportunities are out there for you; take the journey step by step. Some people are scared to follow their passions because they think the leap of faith is too great, but as I've said, you don't have to do it all at once.

Another issue that clients regularly raise with me is that they simply don't have the time to quit their job and find something they enjoy more. And I always question that. There is *always* time to learn something new. Everybody gets the same 24 hours as the prime minister, so it's just about how you use that time. If you really want to stretch yourself, then spend part of your weekend or take an hour after work to learn a new skill. There is always time and there is always a way to try something new.

The only thing keeping you in an unhappy position is your thinking. You are never too old or too busy to grow and you should never sacrifice your mental well-being for easy money. I encourage everyone to find something they love and chase it.

Ironically, one of the reasons people resist making beneficial changes to their lives is because they worry about failing. This has as much to do with fear of stepping outside their comfort zone as it does with perfectionism. A lot of us are stuck because we feel what's the point of bothering when we already know the results won't be perfect. We have no evidence, of course, that this is actually the case, but we convince ourselves that nothing less than perfection is acceptable, therefore what is the point in even trying?

But let me tell you, perfection does not exist. It is a myth and if you think anyone is perfect, it is simply an illusion. I have worked with thousands of clients and I have not met anyone who is perfect yet!

One of the most important and ancient religious texts of Hinduism, the Bhagavad Gita, says: "It is better to live your own destiny imperfectly than to live an imitation of somebody else's life with perfection."

This taps into how brainwashed we are by society's definition of success. We are told repeatedly what success is supposed to look like – reinforced by endless photoshopped images on social media. Mostly, it involves the acquisition of wealth and material goods; of fame and power; of the perfect body or the ideal partner.

It's little wonder then that we often end up chasing goals that have been set by others and eventually feel stuck or frustrated because we realise deep-down that we are not being true to ourselves.

In order to fully realise your potential, you need to ask yourself thought-provoking questions that help you to get to know yourself and challenge any belief that is not in your best interests.

By changing your thoughts, questioning why you're doing what you're doing, and being willing to take the steps –

starting with baby ones – to help you achieve what you really want in life, you will gradually become unstuck.

CASE STUDY

A client came to see me because she felt 'stuck'. When I asked her to talk about the details of why she felt stuck, it emerged that she felt she couldn't speak socially to colleagues at work. It might not sound much but to her it had become a huge problem, because she wanted to interact more with her colleagues but was tongue-tied by fear. Why was she so scared? Because she thought she had nothing to say for herself. She also thought that she knew everyone thought she was stupid and unfriendly.

How did she know this? I asked her. Had they said this to her? Had anyone ever said anything of the sort to her, or about her? Could she read their minds? How, in short, did she know that what she was thinking was the truth? Slowly, she began to see that what she was thinking was only her own perception of the situation; what her mind was telling her. She was effectively paralysed by her own thoughts, but she had no evidence to prove that they were true.

Once she understood that you can't do other people's thinking for them, I was able to help her to work on how to change the way she thought, and to realise that she DID have plenty to say for herself. When I asked her what she had done in the past week, it turned out that she had been to a yoga class, she had tried a new recipe, she had seen a controversial new film... she had loads to say for herself; she only thought she didn't.

What can we all learn from her story? That you have to be careful how you think about things. Your mind is very powerful, and can easily persuade you that certain negative thoughts are true even when they are nothing of the sort.

WORKSHEET

Here's a flow chart to help you change your thoughts.

It's not easy to just 'change a thought', particularly if you think that you are justified in holding on to it.

The key thing to understand is that you are creating your own pain by choosing the thoughts that you are choosing.

You don't HAVE to change the way you think. You could stay as you are. But the negative thoughts that you are holding on to may not be your best choice.

Finding a new thought to replace the old one may feel stupid or bizarre, like trying to force your right foot into your left shoe. Your mind will be unwilling, and may run away from the idea. See if you can persuade it to contemplate the idea of a new thought. Ask, 'what if... I viewed my situation from a different angle?'

In order for the new thought to settle in and take hold, it has to be something that feels better than the old thought. This may require a bit of imagination at first but go with it; have a play, try it on for size.

The new thought also needs to be something you truly believe. That, too, can seem tricky at first.

But if you are willing to try, and open to the idea of thinking differently, it can be done and you will find it is the most powerful tool imaginable.

So, when you are ready, here's how to do it:

FLOW CHART

What is your current painful thought?

_____

_____

Why are you choosing to think this?

_____

_____

How could you think differently about the situation?

_____

_____

What evidence can you find to support your new thought?

_____

_____

How does your new thought make you feel?

_____

_____

CHAPTER FIVE

HOW TO STOP PROCRASTINATING

Do you find yourself procrastinating over the smallest things?

We've all been guilty of procrastination at some point or other in our lives. Putting something off is part of being human, after all. It doesn't matter who you are. You might have reached the pinnacle of your profession – as a judge or hedge fund manager – but that doesn't mean you're immune from procrastination in other areas of your life. America's founding father Benjamin Franklin famously coined the saying, "Don't put off until tomorrow what you can do today", which remains as relevant today as when he first uttered the immortal phrase three centuries ago.

We can find similar calls to action from celebrated writers such as Gabriel Garcia Marquez, who said: "He who awaits much can expect little", and Hunter S. Thompson, who declared: "A man who procrastinates in his choosing will inevitably have his choice made for him by circumstance."

So, what does it mean to procrastinate? Procrastination is the act of unnecessarily postponing decisions or actions. We all know how easy it is to start scrolling through Instagram or surfing the internet in order to avoid finishing a particular task, especially something we consider to be arduous or boring. In the same way, most of us have probably been guilty of procrastination at times when our goals are vague or abstract rather than concrete and clearly defined. For instance, if you simply say you want to get fit but have no real exercise plan, then you are likely to procrastinate. Conversely, if you book a gym class or Zoom fitness session, then your plan is concrete and you are more likely to achieve your goal. Also, we can all feel overwhelmed at times by seemingly impossibly large tasks, but once broken down into manageable, smaller tasks, they don't feel nearly so daunting.

Most of the time, procrastination has no long-term repercussions but, if it becomes a bad habit, it can stop us from achieving our goals: we can fail to reach our potential at school or in the work place. It can impact our relationships and our reputational standing, too, if we are seen to be unreliable and indecisive as a result. An interesting example of how a person in a position of authority can be impacted by indecision is Boris Johnson. His apparent indecisiveness as prime minister during the coronavirus crisis led to internal wrangling within his government and even emboldened some MPs to openly question whether he was fit for the job.

In Johnson's case, it could be argued that the more options he was presented with in terms of how to deal with the pandemic, the harder it was for him to evaluate them and make the right decision. Also, it stands to reason that the greater the consequences of a decision, as in the prime minister's situation, the harder, therefore, it must be to commit to one.

It may seem like procrastination is simply a matter of exercising one's willpower but it's a bit more complicated than that.

Usually, we rely on our self-control and discipline to get something done but what if our motivation isn't there or we can't see the long-term benefits of our efforts? When we're feeling demotivated, combined with contributory factors such as exhaustion and a sense of disconnect with our future self, then our willpower can quickly go out the window and we can end up procrastinating indefinitely. It's not uncommon to engage in activities that bring short-term rewards rather than focus on tasks that would lead to better results in the long term. If the rewards for our actions appear too far in the future, it may seem easier to put off making the effort in the first place. Equally, we may delay studying for an exam until the last minute because the importance of attaining a good grade might not seem so apparent when it's months away.

There are many reasons why people procrastinate, ranging from laziness and sensation-seeking to anxiety and depression. But one of the major causes of serious procrastination is a fundamental fear of failure alongside good old, perfectionism. At its worst, procrastination can become so debilitating it can start to affect a person's entire life, both personal and professional. Plenty of clients have come to my office with stories of how overwhelming fear has led them to constant procrastination, paralysing them from achieving their goals. They convince themselves that whatever work they are planning on doing is not going to be good enough;

it will not be 'perfect', so they say to themselves, "I'm better off not doing it at all".

So, why do people continue to procrastinate even though they know it's bad for them?

If you suffer from low self-esteem and low self-confidence, then you are more likely to experience a fear of failure, and therefore, be more prone to procrastination. If you're constantly afraid to fail, you're more likely to feel incapable of tackling a particular task or assignment – unlike other more confident colleagues or friends for whom fear of failure may act as a spur to get something done. You may think it's easier to put off doing something but, ultimately, you are making the problem worse. Coming up with endless excuses not to act – whether making a life-changing decision or doing something as mundane as paying the bills – only compounds your sense of failure and stops you from moving forward.

DARE TO FAIL

For some of my clients, the prospect of failure is the worst thing in the whole world; as if it is going to ruin their entire life, which I find so interesting because I don't actually believe in 'failure', as such. What I do wholeheartedly believe in is growth – and the only way we can grow is by embracing the opportunities that come our way, however scary or intimidating they might first appear.

What I'm here to tell you is to not be afraid to put yourself out there and learn from your failures. You cannot allow the fear of perceived failure to hold you back. And we are only able to grow through accepting failure and learning from the mistakes we make along the way. But, if we are held back by our fear of failure and it stops us from even trying, then that's when we really will fail. I can tell you from my own experience that every time I have chosen to jump straight in, whether setting up my own business or opting to take a different direction in my life, I have felt myself visibly grow from within. When I embarked on my own self-development, I learnt many, many tough but life-enhancing lessons. So many situations didn't work out as I had planned – and, yes, there were those painful moments of feeling fed up and frustrated - but everything I experienced only ever helped me rise bigger, better, faster and stronger. I found the more I embraced my mistakes, the more confident I became. In other words, I wouldn't have got to where I am now without those lessons. They challenged me to think differently.

We all know that life can be challenging and there is no point in wishing it wasn't. But we can choose to see challenges as propellers of growth, so I say to myself, "Bring it on". When you put yourself out there and allow yourself to be seen, you never know where life might take you. As the saying goes: "There are people less qualified than you, doing the things you want to do, simply because they decide to believe in themselves. Period." If you constantly come up with excuses - for example, telling yourself you're too busy to turn that brilliant business idea into a reality – the only one left on the starting blocks will be you. Phrases like 'tough times' or 'hard days' are all in the mind; it's how you let them impact you is what really counts. Am I having a tough time or is it just a tough five minutes? What am I learning? How can I grow? All of these things lead to new opportunities.

However, if you want to berate yourself for 'failing', then go ahead, be my guest! And you will find yourself going around in circles, not feeling great at all and learning a grand total of nil. Alternatively, if you want to challenge your thinking and ask yourself, "What did I learn here", you will discover an amazing lesson; a new path and will start to feel a lot better.

Once you've changed your mindset about the word failure, you need to recognise that you may fail many times before you achieve the level of success you are seeking. And that is a good thing because failure is not the opposite of success, it is part of success. And success, as we all know, takes time and effort. Ask just about any famous person if they have ever experienced failure in pursuit of their dreams and chances are they will regale you with countless stories of missteps and disasters along the way. Britain's most celebrated leader Sir Winston Churchill once famously exhorted an audience to "never give in". He is also credited with declaring: "Success is going from failure to failure without losing your enthusiasm."

In the same vein, Thomas Edison, America's greatest inventor, is held up as a master of trial and error. When asked about the many thousands of failures he endured while trying to invent the light-bulb more than 150 years ago, he announced, "I have not failed. I've just found 10,000 ways that won't work.". A more contemporary example is Michael Jordan, arguably the world's greatest basketball player, who was spurred to persevere with his sport after being cut from his high school team. As he once said: "I have missed more than 9000 shots in my career. I have lost almost 300 games. On 26 occasions, I have been entrusted to take the game-winning shot, and I missed. I have failed over and over and over again in my life. And that is why I succeed."

TAKE A CHANCE

It's your choice, though. If you keep putting off a decision or deadline, you are ultimately hurting yourself and creating your own pain. If you have something hanging over your head, it can magnify over time and become overwhelming. If you wind yourself up, you are being unkind to yourself for no real reason. Self-discipline is a form of self-care.

One of the best things you will realise is that you are never as bad as you think you may be, and most people won't belittle you for failure. Fear of failure is often fear of the unknown and sometimes it is simply about taking a leap of faith. Stepping outside our comfort zone is, by definition, uncomfortable, but it's often what leads to the greatest success and gives us the most satisfaction – not to mention peace of mind - once we are able to overcome that fear. We can then go on to achieve our goals or even surpass them.

Again, it's our thought processes that we need to examine here. Procrastination is an action created by a negative thought; by thinking you might fail, you create the non-action through that thought process. But what is the worst-case scenario here? It's usually all in your head. If you have the chance to make a point during a company presentation and don't speak up because you are afraid of getting it wrong, the only person you are disadvantaging is yourself.

We sometimes procrastinate because we worry about receiving negative feedback from others, but in many cases, our fears turn out to be unjustified or exaggerated. Chances are, the response might even be positive or at the very least, not as negative as we expect. It stands to reason that if you are thinking the thought "I will fail", this is bound to create a lot of negative feelings. Instead, start to question that thought; ask yourself, is this thought about fear of failure serving me well or making me feel worse? Is this thought going to get me to the feelings and the results I want? Of course, it won't, in which case it is time to start questioning how to think about the situation differently and in a more positive way that will enable you to stop procrastinating. For instance, you might be able to start viewing all feedback as inherently constructive rather than automatically assuming the worst or wasting time worrying unnecessarily about what other people think.

Another example is to create a scenario in your mind whereby you have achieved your goal and not been held back by fear of failure, and think to yourself: "If I hadn't taken the plunge and done that course, I wouldn't have learnt what I am learning now" or "this thing that has happened has taught me about contrast and I have learnt what I don't want in order to know what I now do want."

It is also useful to remember our thoughts are not facts. What we think is a fact is often just a thought. Be mindful of what is a fact and what is a thought and be prepared to challenge yourself to think about things differently. It can feel very isolating when you believe that you are the only one in the world who feels afraid to act. But the truth is that these thoughts and feelings are not uncommon so it is really important to open up to friends and loved ones as talking about things can help you to feel better right away and get you seeing things from a clearer, more realistic perspective. And never forget, everyone has to fail, to win.

Fear of failure often goes hand-in-hand with anxiety and perfectionism. The more anxious you are, the more likely you are to procrastinate, which then becomes a self-perpetuating loop. Equally, if you are a perfectionist, you might become so worried about making a mistake that you end up not doing the task at hand. In your quest to produce a flawless piece of work, you might constantly delay finishing it, thereby putting your job, university degree or even relationships in jeopardy. If often follows that the bigger and more important the assignment, the greater the degree of procrastination.

So many of my clients and students decide not to do things because they want everything to be perfect. They avoid speaking up or putting themselves forward in case they "get it wrong". In their desire to get everything right all the time, they often end up procrastinating or hiding themselves or their amazing talent from everyone in order to ensure they don't make mistakes. But being perfect all the time is just not humanly possible – or desirable. I've personally found that the more my business has grown and the greater my workload - from coaching to public speaking - the more I have also accepted that I'm never going to be perfect. And nor do I want to be.

SELF-SABOTAGE

Another reason why people procrastinate is due to their tendency to engage in self-defeating behaviours, which means they actively try to sabotage their own progress. Self-sabotage is when we say that we want something but then go about making sure it doesn't happen – this can either be a conscious or a subconscious process – because we feel we don't deserve the happy ending. So many of us feel guilty about putting ourselves first and going after what we really want, mainly due to how we have been brought up; the society we live in, our culture, belief system, gender etc. We are fed information, often through social media, that means we have to keep pushing harder, working harder, exercising harder, dieting harder, so it's no wonder so many of us don't feel good enough – and are therefore prepared to sabotage our own chances of happiness and/or success.

Some of the main reasons for self-sabotage are fear of failure; an unconscious need to be in control; feeling like you aren't good enough, and fear of success. Signs include making plans and never following through; talking about what you want to do but never actually ever "getting around to it", and procrastinating a lot. Common self-sabotaging behaviours include dating people who are unavailable, accepting jobs which don't reflect your experience, and not being able to say 'no'.

The best way to overcome any type of self-sabotaging behaviour is to first understand your patterns of behaviour and then look for evidence to disprove the thoughts that are creating your indecision or paralysis. For example, look at why you should be in the running for an amazing new job rather than assume you'll never get it. Challenge the hell out of that negativity!

Another self-defeating type of behaviour linked to procrastination is imposter syndrome. So many of us suffer from this modern-day condition. It can happen to anyone at any time, and usually the more responsibility a job holds, the more this syndrome can infect your mind. The thoughts range from "I'm not good enough" to "I'll never be able to do this" to "I'm going to be found out", and the problem is all these thoughts are terrifying and sometimes even physically debilitating.

Funnily enough, the more successful someone is, the more prone they can be to feeling under threat of being "found out" or exposed as a "fraud". Sir Paul McCartney, all-round superstar and one of the world's greatest living musicians, recently hinted that even he suffered from a touch of imposter syndrome. He told Uncut magazine (November 2020) that he was surprised The Beatles were still remembered at all, 50 years on, saying: "I don't quite understand it." He added: "I wish I knew I was Paul McCartney; it would be so much easier. You can achieve a lot of fame but we're all a bit fragile inside. Everyone has this, 'Should I? Shouldn't I?'. Even the biggest braggarts, guys who you would think never worry about a thing, when you get to know them a bit more, you realise they're just like the rest of us."

At its core, this syndrome is a form of anxiety - and fear is the fuel to the fire. Anxiety is created by your thinking, and I want you start thinking more powerfully and in line with who you really are, if you find yourself procrastinating - for example, about whether to accept a promotion or apply for a better-paid, more fulfilling job. Basically, you need to reframe your thoughts and realise that what you're feeling isn't founded on anything real. Feelings of inadequacy and fear are all in your mind, so imagine how you would feel if you could turn those thoughts into something positive. Instead of thinking along the lines of, "I don't know *anything*", why not try reframing it to "I don't know *everything*...yet. I'm still learning?".

See how it feels when you don't put the pressure on yourself to know it all. As I continually say, no one is perfect, so learn to take mistakes in your stride and view them as a natural part of the process. There will never be the "perfect time," and your work will never be 100% flawless. The sooner you're able to accept that, the better off you'll be.

Take a look at all the evidence you already have as to why you *can* do the job, why you *can* handle responsibility and why you *can* cope well under pressure. I promise you, when you start looking for evidence to back up the positive you will find it. You just need to look.

Start now by recounting your most recent accomplishments. Take a look at everything you've achieved, and reflect on all the hard work you've put in to get to where you are now.

Embrace the fact that you got yourself to where you are. You've earned your place and your accomplishments are proof of that. Don't torment yourself with self-doubt about whether you can do the job or not, because your bosses have already made it clear they believe in you and your skills by employing you in the first place! You did not pull a fast one on anyone. You did not lie and cheat your way into this promotion or position. Don't doubt the intelligence of those who hired you; they have made deliberate choices based on your experience and potential. You really do deserve to be there. When you start to act 'as if' you do deserve a pay rise, a new job or a distinction for a university assignment, and know that you can do it and will be amazing at it, then it's very likely that this will be the outcome. Sometimes you have to 'fake it to make it' and that can bring with it a wonderful confidence.

Procrastination can be easily resolved. Figuring out the underlying causes of your procrastination is crucial - but you need to be honest with yourself if you want to be able to successfully overcome it. Once you've done this, you can formulate a plan of action.

Writing can be one of the most therapeutic ways to identify and fix your problems. I find it works especially well when you are retraining yourself to not procrastinate. One of my favourite sayings is: "Your thinking creates what you are feeling, and what you are feeling creates what you do." Writing out how you feel and what you may think is wrong can help you to identify what's holding you back and help to start fixing the problem.

CASE STUDY

I had one particular client who came to see me to try to overcome his procrastination about ending a toxic relationship as well as his self-sabotage and anxiety issues around food. He felt his life was not moving forward. We did some work together to help him change his thinking and in turn propel him into action. He sent me this email about a year later....

"Hi Jacqueline, I'm in the process of moving out of my flat so having a spring clean along the way. I've found the notebook you gave me when I first came to see you and I didn't want to open it because I knew the thoughts and feelings from back then were almost entirely negative. I had a glance and ceremonially tore up the pages. It was amusing how those issues holding me back are so insignificant now. As well as helping me take back control of my thoughts around the toxic relationship I will be eternally grateful to you for helping me overcome my anxiety issues. I knew they were limiting my life but I chose to accept those parameters rather than address them. It's not being over dramatic to say the work we did when I first came to see you absolutely changed my life. I know there will always be challenges in life, however, the debilitating anxiety around food and dating has well and truly gone."

Quitting the habit of smoking is something many people procrastinate about incessantly, sometimes for years. Overcoming an addiction can be frightening but we all know that smoking, along with other addictions like drugs and alcohol, can be dangerous. One of my clients continually put off trying to kick the habit until we started to talk about what was making him fearful of stopping and he started to change his thinking around it. You can't change the action without looking at the why and how. This client suffered from shortness of breath and other health issues, and finally, he came up with his own thinking about why the long-term damage he was doing to himself by continuing to smoke far outweighed the short-term buzz he got from it.

WORKSHEET:

Buy a journal or diary and get organised. Self-discipline is often the first step towards overcoming procrastination!

Recognise your behaviour and write down the thoughts that are holding you back i.e., fear of ridicule, embarrassment, fear of failure. What is going on in your head that is telling you to take zero action? Try to be reflective and honest with yourself.

_____

_____

_____

_____

Next, write down what your life is like with procrastination and what it could be like without it. For example, if your house is full of clutter but you can't face clearing it, do you feel happy or frustrated? How would you feel if you tackled that clutter? Would it make you lighter, happier, more productive?

_____

_____

_____

_____

Reward yourself if you do something you didn't really want to do – i.e., if you tackle your tax return, treat yourself to an organic take-away coffee or take a short break to read an interesting article or scroll through Instagram.

List down the way you will reward yourself.

_____

_____

_____

_____

Divide tasks into small steps - you don't have to do the whole thing in one massive hit!

Prioritise what is and isn't important.

CHAPTER SIX:

HOW TO MANAGE YOUR STRESS LEVELS AND FIND BALANCE

Do you find it hard to handle stress? (By the way, stress need not be a bad thing!)

If you look back at recent conversations with friends, colleagues and loved ones, how many of them - when you've asked how they are - have responded with "Urgh, stressed"? Probably most, I would imagine.

It's extremely common to be stressed in today's fast-paced, ultra-connected world. In fact, a staggering 79% of employed British adults experience work-related stress, according to a 2020 survey of nearly 2000 people by London human resource consultancy Perkbox. This makes it the most common form of stress in the UK – and it's on the rise, up 20 percent compared to the findings of a 2018 survey, which questioned a similar number of employed Britons. The second most common form of stress is financial/monetary with 60 percent of adults experiencing this, while family stress is third with 48 percent, followed by health-related stress (45 percent) and relationship stress (35 percent).

It's no surprise, therefore, to learn that people's mental health is suffering big time. According to a Mental Health Foundation study in 2018, a total of 74 percent of people were so stressed they felt overwhelmed or unable to cope.

That's millions of people at risk of seriously damaging their health.

As human beings, we aren't wired physically or mentally to deal with the modern information overload that we're bombarded with on a daily basis. We're also expected to be contactable 24/7 – with access via the touch of a button on our smart phones or other digital devices. As a result, many of us are unable to ever switch off and find balance in our lives.

There is no doubt that stress is one of the great public health challenges of our time, which is why it is more important than ever to understand what is causing us personal stress and learning what steps we can take to reduce it for ourselves and those around us.

So, what is stress? Stress is ultimately when we go into what is called 'fight-or-flight' mode, where the body and mind release a battery of stress hormones, including cortisol, to enable us to cope with danger or emergencies. A managed amount of stress is essential for our survival. However, when we suffer from chronic stress, cortisol continually floods our bloodstream, putting us at serious risk of mental burnout. It can cause us to feel completely overwhelmed, exhausted, irritable, resentful and hopeless. Like we're on an out-of-control, malfunctioning hamster wheel and can't get off.

As well as being a significant factor in mental health problems including anxiety and depression if left unchecked, stress is also linked to physical health issues like heart disease, a compromised immune system, insomnia, digestive problems, muscular tensions, aches and pains, and headaches. Other symptoms can include panic attacks and obsessive-compulsive behaviour.

FRESH PERSPECTIVE

Stress starts in the mind and then impacts on the physical. Not the other way around. It's about the mind first. I teach my clients and students that stress can be banished from our lives by learning how to think right. Stress is an emotion that can be changed via our thinking: how we think creates how we feel and that generates the actions we take, so we must start to look at our own thoughts first and foremost.

Ultimately, no one can make you feel anything; you create your feelings from your thoughts, and choosing thoughts that create stress is painful for you and you only. Remember, when we blame others we create a lot of stress for ourselves, which is why we need to learn how to think differently in order to feel calmer. That is, of course, if calm is your preferred feeling!

If you are feeling stressed, the first thing to do is to write down your thoughts – get them out of your head and onto paper. It makes them more tangible. Now examine those thoughts. Are the thoughts you're choosing helpful or hurtful? If it's the latter, start to find a fresh perspective and focus on breaking destructive habits.

Let's say you are tasked with preparing a presentation for work. If you are thinking, "I can't do this", it's more likely you will be feeling stressed. Instead, you need to start thinking more constructively about the job in hand to create a different feeling. Challenge yourself by looking at it from the opposite perspective; in other words, start to look for evidence to prove to yourself why you absolutely CAN do it. It won't be easy at first, but just as a muscle develops with the right exercise, your mind will develop, too.

Once you understand that it is your thinking that generates your feelings and that you have a choice as to how you think, your life will change dramatically. As the American self-help and spiritual author Dr Wayne Dyer once said: "If you change the way you look at things, the things you look at change." The way we spot, view and react to stress can be one of the hardest cycles to break but it can be done once you understand all your feelings are within your control. And also realise that there is no point trying to control things that are beyond your control as that is what causes stress and anxiety in the first place! Another saying I hold dear, which I learnt when I was in recovery, is: "Grant me the serenity to accept the things I cannot change, the courage to change the things I can, and the wisdom to know the difference." I love this because it is so simple and yet so powerful.

Once you've grasped these essential truths, the things that you used to allow to bother you will simply not affect you anymore. A lot of this is about learning to let go of the things you cannot control…

It's also important to teach yourself to become willing to feel any emotion. Everything we avoid in life is because we are afraid of how it will make us feel. Yet if we are willing to feel any emotion then we can go into absolutely any situation with very little fear and there will be nothing that we can't do. I remember when I was recovering from anorexia, I had a massive fear of putting on even half a pound, but I also knew that if I didn't put on weight, I would never recover. I had to overcome the fear by thinking thoughts that were helpful – not harmful. I had to change how I thought in order to feel calm, instead of stressed out. The main thought I chose was, "If not now, when?". It was powerful and made me push forward in my recovery. Whenever I felt the fear I knew I had to work on my thoughts and when I did that, I would feel a lot better.

It's no coincidence that people who become hugely successful and famous will have often overcome serious adversity – and stress - to achieve their goals. They will have faced their fears to the extent that their overall attitude towards life is "Bring it on". Take American style maven and former J. Crew creative director Jenna Lyons, who launched a line of false eyelashes called LoveSeen in 2020. This was very much a personal venture for Lyons, who was born with a rare genetic disorder called Bloch-Sulzberger syndrome or incontinentia pigmenti (IP), which can cause skin scarring, loss of hair and malformed teeth. Although she has the milder form, the condition left her with enough visible signs – she has only seven eyelashes and wears dentures – to make her acutely aware growing up of how different she looked compared to other children. 'I was officially gross. Not my outfit. Not my hairstyle. Me. I, Jenna Lyons, was gross," she has said.

Did she let her disorder ruin her life, though? No. Having faced all those emotions associated with feeling bad about herself, she used them to empower herself, saying in an interview: "…I had no choice except to put one foot in front of the other and keep going. And to this day, I often feel like I'm on the outside. But what I realised along the way was that a lot of the really smart, interesting, talented, compassionate and equally dysfunctional people sit out here with me." Now she's putting her energies into helping others through her brand.

WAKE-UP CALL

As strange as it may sound, there can be a positive flipside to stress. I strongly believe that being aware you are 'stressed' can actually be good for you because it's a signal that you can either carry on doing what you are doing and getting the same results or you can wake up to the fact that something in your life needs to change urgently. Stress could be the pivotal factor which allows you to make a change for the better.

Some time ago, I found myself in hospital undergoing an MRI scan for my brain. I'd been suffering from severe migraine headaches, which I'd never experienced before so immediately feared the worst and assumed I had a tumour or some other brain-related illness. Afterwards, the consultant gave me the news that my brain was absolutely healthy and the migraine diagnosis was because I was suffering from stress.

It was a huge wake-up call for me. When I looked back, it was clear I'd been caught in the middle of a perfect storm of life events that left me feeling exhausted and overwhelmed. I was going through an extremely acrimonious divorce from my ex-husband; I'd moved house and was renovating a new apartment, and, to top it all, the builders I had employed turned out to be cowboys. I was also continuing to work full time. To sum up, I was juggling a lot but in typical Type A-personality fashion, I thought I was just "getting on with it".

As soon as I became aware that I was, indeed, suffering from stress, I left hospital vowing not to play that game again; of thinking that I had to do it all, right here, right now. I calmed my mind down immediately and changed the way I was thinking about everything pretty much instantly. Instead of telling myself that I had to keep pushing on and getting it all done, I adjusted my mindset to think, "I don't have to do it all now" – as well as, "This will eventually get done; it won't not get done". It worked at once.

Being in the eye of the storm can understandably cause our inner forecasts to hit some serious turbulence. However, remembering the wider picture often acts as a pacifying first step. Sometimes it's good to step back and ask yourself, "Is that going to make any difference in ten years' time?". Ninety per cent of the time, the answer is no. It's sometimes a matter of putting the problems you face into perspective and accepting that most of the things we worry about are not life-or-death issues. When we try to mentally shrink what's worrying us, our problems often don't seem like such a big deal after all.

Singer Gary Barlow recently revealed that he used to be consumed by a feeling of dread when his band Take That was at its height during the 1990s. Despite the accolades and the fame, he wasn't able to enjoy his success. When the band reformed in the 2000s, he approached it with a different mindset, telling Metro newspaper (27/11/2020): "I thought, 'I'm not going to worry this time'. The worrying at night doesn't get you any further forward the next day. I don't do that anymore." With the benefit of hindsight, he was able to take that crucial step back and avoid burnout a second time round. He achieved this via his thinking and his thinking alone – in other words, the situation didn't change, just his way of thinking about it did.

Like many alpha personalities, Barlow is a classic over-achiever/perfectionist. During the coronavirus pandemic, the number of people who reported feeling high levels of stress and anxiety rose sharply, with many working longer hours while looking after school children at home or caring for elderly relatives – or both. Combined with the seismic shift to working from home, it was inevitable that the boundaries between work and personal life became seriously blurred. This was a particular issue for over-achievers, who found it more difficult than ever to switch off.

If you're a perfectionist or people-pleaser, you are more prone to high levels of stress or burnout than those who are able to say 'no', which makes it vital that you learn how to cut yourself some slack.

Listen to the way you talk to yourself; often you'll find you're harder on yourself than anyone else, convincing yourself that you haven't done enough or aren't good enough. Equally, your expectations are more likely to be way higher than you would set them for anyone else. As our own worst critics, we tend to kick ourselves even more when we're down, leading to greater feelings of stress, anxiety and low self-esteem.

But if you asked yourself how you would talk to a friend in this situation, would you be yelling at her that she will never get it sorted out or is an idiot to have got herself into that situation? Or would you treat her with kindness and love? Exactly! So, when you really understand this, you will choose to treat yourself nicely and be kinder with your thoughts - and your stress will gradually disappear.

LEARN TO SAY 'NO'

Women, in particular, are tough on themselves; they are programmed to take on the burden of caring for everyone else while often forgetting to look after themselves. It's no surprise that during the first weeks of the UK lockdown (26 March to 26 April 2020), women carried out an average of two-thirds more childcare duties per day than men, according to the Office for National Statistics (ONS) data. They also spent more time on unpaid work and less time on paid work than men.

Change sometimes starts with learning how to say 'no' – I learnt this pretty quickly in my own career. Six months after I started my life coaching business, I booked into a spa hotel for a weekend and slept for 14 hours straight. I was exhausted from working round the clock and not looking after myself properly. It was exhilarating building my clinic and my client-base grew quickly, but because I wanted to help my clients, I always said 'yes' when they wanted to see me – at all times of day or night. It wasn't in my nature to say 'no'.

Again, that lost weekend of sleep was my wake-up call. I remember thinking, "This is not balance", and realised I needed to practice what I preached! I started going in to my office later and made sure I finished by 7pm. I took Fridays off and I learnt how to tell clients I couldn't see them that day but could make an appointment for the following week. To my utter surprise, they were totally fine with that and my lesson was learnt! My business continued to thrive while I managed to get my life back.

Unfortunately, so many of us don't believe that we're worthy of self-care. Of course, we are worthy of taking care of ourselves! I learnt this very important lesson when I embarked on getting clean 18 years ago; I realised that I had to practice self-care in order to learn discipline, kindness and compassion - as much for myself as others.

If we are to guard against stress or burnout, it's important to switch off – but the more stressed we become the harder this is to achieve. Learning how to give our mind a break takes practice. We also need to find ways to relax that are easily achievable. I constantly see clients who feel as though they are overworked, particularly City workers, but that's only because they don't take enough time for themselves. When I tell them they need to prioritise taking time out for themselves, they automatically respond that they would love to go on holiday but could never find the time to do that. They then start to worry about how they are going to manage to shoe-horn a holiday into their hectic schedule. But - as I tell them - it doesn't have to mean a week-long break in the Maldives, as enticing as that sounds! It's simply about creating a space and time in their day or night to simply stop and take a deep breath.

Balance comes in the form of joy – anything you find joyful could be part of your 'balance'. My top tip is to schedule time in your diary to switch off – literally call it switch-off time. And don't be afraid to spend some time alone. Take a hot bath, read a book, cook some nourishing food, exercise – and most importantly, turn off your iPhone/iPad and any other electronic devises.

This may seem like common sense, but you would be surprised by how many people forget to do it. Recharging your batteries and breaking away from your desk is just as important as working hard at your job.

One quote that really resonates with me is, "You can't pour from an empty cup", which means if you push yourself to the point of exhaustion, you won't be able to function in the long run. If you keep giving and giving and giving, you will soon have nothing left to give. That is not balance.

FINDING BALANCE

If you take even ten minutes out of your day to make sure your mental health is on track, then you will find your happiness and productivity will gradually improve.

Another factor which can make it difficult for people to jump off that racing hamster wheel, is the tendency to confuse self-worth with materialistic wealth. In today's society, we are brainwashed into believing that happiness can only be achieved through materialistic means or other external sources.

We are conditioned into thinking that if we buy certain cars; are on special diets to achieve a certain body shape or size, or if we buy certain products, like clothes, jewellery, homes etc, only then will we feel happy and fulfilled. This is exacerbated by social media, which is basically a highlight reel of people's lives and not at all an authentic representation of their day-to-day existence, which can be fraught with the same worries and insecurities as the rest of us.

As a result, we develop unrealistic expectations of how we think our lives should look and put ourselves under undue pressure.

The truth is, happiness has nothing to do with your perceived status in life; how much you earn, who you're married to, what kind of job you have or who your extended family are. It has nothing to do with anything that is outside of you. The Dalai Lama tells us, "Happiness is not something ready-made, it comes from your own actions." This is the point I'm trying to make - that it doesn't matter how nice your life looks online or how many pairs of shoes you have in your closet, happiness isn't something you can go out and buy or wrap yourself up in; these things may bring you temporary fulfilment but I guarantee, it will soon fade. Happiness is something unique to the individual; created by you internally. You have to find it via your mind.

This was brought home during the coronavirus crisis when many people took the opportunity to press pause on their frantic lifestyles and reassess their priorities. Faced with a situation that was entirely out of their control, i.e., a global pandemic, and all the uncertainty and fear associated with that, they looked at what they could control and that was their own state of mind. For many, particularly those who made the shift to working from home, this triggered a reappraisal of urban living with increasing numbers leaving the cities in search of green space and a more balanced lifestyle. According to Rightmove, the UK's largest online property website, there was a 126 percent increase in people considering properties in village locations in 2020, with the biggest rise in sales in seaside resorts. This showed that given the chance to stop, people were able to take stock and make conscious decisions about wanting to live better lives.

This doesn't surprise me at all. I'm a big believer in nature and I've always had dogs in my life for that reason. When I was attending back-to-back AA meetings at the start of my recovery, I would make a point of going for walks in-between in Hyde Park and I did a lot of my healing there. To this day, I still do that and it always helps me to realise how unimportant many of the things are that cause us to become stuck. Walking in nature also reminds me that change and growth are beautiful things and to never take life too seriously.

HELPFUL TIPS

I want to share with you a few tips that I find really help me to feel more balanced:

FIRST, it's about getting active (especially in nature): We spend most of our time at work, sitting down, yet we are not designed to sit in a chair all day. Neither are we designed to be inside all day long. Taking some cardiovascular exercise probably has the biggest impact on mood and reducing stress but don't overdo it! If you thrash yourself at the gym after work, you'll only increase the stress on an already stressed system. But it's really hard to still feel stressed after a long walk in nature. Spending time in nature reconnects us with our natural environment and helps to balance our mood.

SECOND, pick a self-care practice that works for you. Committing to regular meditation or yoga or listening to spiritual YouTube clips, can help you to remain calm, feel less stressed and be more joyful - even in the midst of chaos. Find something each day that brings you back to you. Many of my clients opt for mindfulness meditation because it gives you conscious control over your thoughts by requiring you to be fully present in the moment via your senses. It allows you – through controlled breathing - to calmly observe your thoughts and feelings from a distance and without judgment. You can practise by sitting still, doing forms of yoga such as hatha, or while carrying out mundane tasks such as washing up. Devote five minutes or 50 – whatever you like – to it each day, and I guarantee, you will gain clarity, perspective and a sense of calm. Personally, I love listening to something spiritual each night before bed. I turn on YouTube and find anything that takes my fancy, from spiritual teacher Eckhart Tolle to self-help author and motivational speaker Wayne Dyer, and listen as I drift off to sleep. It is a powerful practice that I live by.

THIRD, I make a point of practising gratitude. Another favourite saying of mine is you cannot be grateful and depressed at the same time. And it is so true! Gratitude is a massive help in challenging your mindset. Making time each day to appreciate all you have to be grateful for enables you to shift your focus away from your fears to the positives in your life and solutions to your problems. Rather than compare ourselves with those we consider to be more fortunate, give a thought, instead, to those who experience hardship every day, like refugees in a refugee camp. Be grateful for the small things – legs to walk, eyes to see, a roof over your head – and start to feel thankful. You can't feel bad while you're feeling thankful. Gratitude is the antidote to fear, anxiety and depression. It takes practice and it might feel a bit strange at the start but I promise you, if you practise it daily, you will see your life and your feelings change.

AND FINALLY, make time for fun and friends. It's sometimes good for us to take a moment and stop being so serious. Whether paying our bills, doing our job or rushing to catch our train on time, life is serious and full of responsibilities, stress and deadlines. When was the last time you jumped in a puddle or just took some time out to relax or take up a hobby, just for the fun of it? When we take life too seriously and feel in a state of constant stress, we begin to lose touch with what makes life so great in the first place – having fun! Life is meant to be enjoyed, yet I constantly meet people who have forgotten that. You will be surprised by how much better you will feel if you allow yourself to relax and just do something simple and silly.

With loneliness on the rise thanks to the impact of the coronavirus lockdowns and other societal factors (more than seven million people reported feeling lonely during the first month of 2020 lockdown, according to the Office for National Statistics), it's more important than ever to connect with other people. But choose your friends wisely. I'm a big believer in having open and honest communication with friends who are equally conscious, aware and awake. I'm very careful about who I spend my time with because my time is so precious. I'm happy with my own company and don't need others to entertain me, but my small group of good girlfriends are vital to my wellbeing. They make me happy and less stressed. Remember to trust your instincts. When people walk out of your life, consider that a good thing because it opens up space for you to accept new, more meaningful friendships that add value to your life.

CASE STUDY

I had one amazing woman come to see me because she was super stressed and kept agreeing to do everything for everyone and anyone. She was in her 30s with two children, working full-time in banking and found it very difficult to ever say 'no'. She was so exhausted from juggling multiple demands on her time and energy that she told me she felt "broken". When we talked about what was going on in her life, it was clear that her biggest issue was her inability to say 'no'. She had a fear of letting people down, being disliked and not being the "best". We did some work together and I taught her some tools to de-stress via her mindset and boost her self-esteem as a result. We focused on metacognition, which is the ability to reflect and critically analyse how you think so that you can select strategies to tackle challenges more effectively. After just a few sessions, she literally bloomed in front of my eyes. She started feeling more confident; learnt to say 'no' more often; was less stressed and felt freer. Her life really did execute a 180 degree turn in so many ways. She left me a Google review when we had finished, which read: "When I first reached out to Jacqueline, I was broken. My self-esteem was non-existent and my self-loathing ruled the way I lived my life. At our first session, I immediately trusted her, like I had never trusted anyone before. A few months later, and I am a new woman! I can't thank Jacqueline enough for guiding me through this journey of self-discovery, self-acceptance and self-love. She can be tough, but it's tough love that she gives, and cer-

tainly just what I needed. If you really want to change something in your life – and for good – Jacqueline should be your next call or email."

WORKSHEET:

List your top five priorities:

_____

_____

_____

_____

Are you living in line with these?

_____

_____

Why have you chosen these particular priorities?

_____

_____

Are any of them causing you stress and if so, why?

_____

_____

Can you change how you think about any of them, so that you feel calmer?

_____

_____

Do you need to reassess any of them?

_____

_____

What changes do you need to make?

_____

_____

Can you make those changes, just one at a time?

_____

_____

CHAPTER SEVEN

HOW TO ACHIEVE YOUR GOALS AND GET THE RESULTS YOU WANT

Do you want to achieve a goal but don't know how to do it?

We may think that achieving a goal – whether professional, personal, financial or emotional - is simply a matter of carrying out the action necessary to facilitate it. Of course, the action part is crucial but it doesn't start with that; it starts with the mind, our most powerful tool.

Our mind controls how we approach our goal and whether we believe we can achieve it or not. Having the right mindset is key. There are many reasons we may never manage to fulfill our ambitions or objectives; lack of confidence, fear of failure, fear of stepping outside our comfort zones, or other people's negativity. These and other factors can all play a part in stopping us from reaching that often elusive goal.

But what we do know and what many of us have experienced at some point or other, is the buzz we get when we do manage to break through those mind barriers and achieve our objectives. That's our body releasing feel-good hormones like endorphins and dopamine. They provide us with feelings of pleasure and satisfaction when we gain the results we've been striving for. Conversely, when we feel demotivated or unenthusiastic, those hormone levels are correspondingly low.

Let's hold on to those euphoric feelings for a moment as we look at what might be holding us back. Only once we've established our personal roadblocks, will we be ready to move from a negative to a positive thinking pattern and apply goal setting techniques to achieve what we really want in order to live the life we love.

Lack of confidence is often a major factor. Confidence is one of those things that we think others are 'lucky' to have; as though they have this superpower that those with low self-confidence can only dream about. Confident people seem to have it all: they can hold their own in a room, are admired by others, and their positivity and energy seem to promote and inspire confidence in everyone they meet. They come across as people who are at peace with themselves, who face their fears head-on and couldn't care less what anyone else thinks about them. They also tend to be the types who get things done – and succeed in realising their goals. So how does that work? How is it that they are so confident, even if they may be less qualified than you? What is it they have that you think you don't...

The secret is simple: they believe in themselves.

I'm here to tell you that you can boost your confidence and get the results you want, too. As you will discover, it's all a matter of learning how to deal with any pesky negative thoughts and replace them with ones that will make you feel good. If you can reframe your thinking, you'll suddenly find that your confidence will soar. Secondly, pick someone you admire and start to model yourself on that person. For example, if Michelle Obama has the sort of confidence you aspire to and if you are in a situation where you want to be that confident, ask yourself, "What would Michelle do?". Works every time.

But, please don't make the mistake of comparing yourself with someone else. Comparison, as we all know, is the thief of joy and a total time waster. The truth is, you never really know what is going on in other people's lives: the man who appears to have it all might be in severe debt or suffering from anxiety, and the woman who seems happy and successful might be struggling with not being able to have children. Celebrate your own accomplishments and learn to be comfortable in yourself, instead.

In the same way, stop caring about what other people think – because you have absolutely no control over their thoughts. Frankly, most people are not as interested in you and your actions, thoughts, or appearance as you might think they are. As the saying goes, "Those who mind don't matter and those who matter don't mind." If someone (without any expert knowledge) tries to tell you that your plan is unrealistic, understand that they are merely trying to impose their own belief system on you. Your goal might seem unrealistic to them based on their own experiences but that doesn't mean you should be subject to the same mental limitations.

DO YOUR OWN THING

So, just go ahead and do your own thing - and understand that the opinion of you that counts the most, is your own.

Now, we just have to make sure our minds are properly managed so that our thinking patterns can take us in the right direction. When clients say to me they want to achieve a specific goal, I always tell them to come up with between three and five strong thoughts that make them feel good and that will help to empower them to move towards that goal with confidence, resolve and awareness. In other words, they must start to engage in positive thinking of the glass half-full variety by choosing thoughts that support rather than hinder them. The action part will then largely take care of itself.

If you wish to set goals you must be prepared to follow them through, and to do that, it's important to be emotionally invested in the journey; you need to have an emotional connection to what it is you are trying to achieve, otherwise you probably won't feel compelled to stay the course.

For example, let's say you've decided you want to start going to the gym to get fit. You think that by getting fit you'll achieve your goal and your life will be happier and more fulfilled as a result. That's all very well, but you could find that going to the gym doesn't miraculously make you happy, and that's because you haven't approached the challenge of getting fit with the right mindset. Your brain is going to stop the action from achieving the desired result unless you can apply positive meaning to the task in hand. If you aren't fully committed or you don't actually believe you will succeed in getting fit, you won't be able to achieve your goal. You need to look at your mindset first and foremost before embarking on a course of action.

Another way of looking at it is to imagine an army as the 'action' part. It can be ready, willing and able to do battle, but unless it is being led by the right leader, giving the right orders at the right time, such as Winston Churchill during WWII, then that action will be without purpose or direction. The army simply won't be able to function effectively.

But, I hear you ask, how do you manage to think great thoughts, which, in turn, will make you feel more positive and help you to ultimately act? For starters, you have to push yourself. You have to train your mind to believe that by going for a run, for instance, you will feel equally as good whether it's cold and wet or bright and sunny. Try to imagine how you will feel once you have achieved that small fitness goal for the day and know that you are bound to feel immeasurably better and invigorated for it. You could even say to yourself, "I'm so grateful and lucky to be able to run and to have legs that will support me", or "I'm worthy of going on this run and enjoying some self-care."

One incredibly inspirational public figure is four-time Olympic champion Sir Mo Farah, who at the age of 38, aims to make even more Olympic history in his bid to become the first athlete to win the 10,000m in three consecutive Games. He won 5000m and 10,000m gold at both the 2012

London and 2016 Rio Games and intends to defend his 10,000m title at the rescheduled Toyko Olympics.

Although he can already claim to be Britain's most successful ever track athlete, he still thrives on pushing and challenging himself and admits he's "still hungry" to do and achieve more. "It's not because I'm searching for history or to get three gold medals at three different Olympics," he explained in an interview with the Daily Mirror (11/01/2020). "It's because you believe in that and you feel you can still do it. That is what drives me. I will give it 110 percent and that's all I can do. Nothing is guaranteed. But if you don't do it, how are you ever going to know?"

It's been an extraordinary journey for the long-distance icon, who arrived in Britain from war-torn Somalia at the age of eight with little English and a wayward streak. Although naturally talented, Sir Mo puts his success down to hard work and not taking anything for granted. "If someone had said to me [as an eight-year-old boy] that I would win so many medals, be knighted by the Queen and be called Sir Mo Farah – I wouldn't believe any of it," he told BBC Sport (14/09/2020) "It just shows that anything is possible if you work hard."

Similarly, when David Beckham secured his legendary last-minute free-kick against Greece to send the England team to the 2002 World Cup, it might have catapulted him to global stardom and into the realms of celebrity, but his success was hard-earned – and certainly not achieved overnight. He'd already put in the years of hard graft to earn a reputation as one of the best free-kick takers in the world and one of the most diligent trainers, practising over and over again until he had perfected his craft.

FEEL EMPOWERED

It all comes back to mindset. As I always say, if you think you can, you will; if you think you can't, you won't. When clients say to me, "I can't" in relation to why they're not taking the necessary steps towards achieving their goals, my response is to come straight back with the question: "Why would you think that?". Why not reframe the question instead and ask yourself: "What would happen if I could?". Or, "What evidence do I have to prove that I can?". When you start to say "I can", you will start to actually *believe* you can, and in the process, feel empowered.

Thinking positive thoughts will at least allow you to try, which will give you a greater chance of actually reaching your goal. By contrast, saying "I can't" is disempowering, hurtful and so often, just not true.

Fashion designer Bella Freud is hardly the sort of person you would think ever suffered from lack of motivation or confidence. The multi-talented daughter of artist Lucien Freud, she runs a successful international fashion brand and has worked as a writer, producer, director and actress. On the face of it, she appears totally goal-driven. But even she admits to having been trapped at times by her own limiting belief system, saying in an interview with the Evening Standard (25/11/2020): "I used to wonder what is going to happen... now I think, 'How am I going to make this happen?'"

You can only start to make things happen, though, if you are prepared to act on the thoughts and ideas that pop into your head. If you intend to do something but don't actually carry out the action necessary to achieve it, then that intention amounts to no more than wishful thinking. One way to help turn your intentions into something more tangible is to write down your goals. I find that using old-fashioned pen and paper works best because the act of committing something to paper makes you instantly more focused and more invested in your quest.

Interestingly, it's a form of visualisation often employed by famous people to reach their goals. The Hollywood actor Jim Carrey speaks openly about how he wrote himself a cheque for $10 million for "Acting Services Rendered" when he was broke and desperately trying to break into the industry. He dated it Thanksgiving 1995 – and a year or so before that date, he was signed in the lead role of Dumb and Dumber, which went on to gross $247 million at the box office.

When people tell me they can't find the time to pursue their passion project, which might be starting their own business, I always query that. It's about how you use your time that counts. If you really want to do something new, you will find the time. We can all think of a million reasons as to why we won't be able to achieve our goals but these are just excuses. Simply put, if you can't make the time for something, it's clearly not a high enough priority for you.

If you continue to think like that, then, naturally, nothing will change. You will remain stuck in a negative thinking pattern, rather than challenging yourself to look beyond it.

Think about how you want to feel. Do you really want to feel miserable, scared or inadequate because of your inaction? No, of course you don't! If you try to think consciously and mindfully about the feeling that inspired you to want to build your own business in the first place, you'll probably realise it was one of excitement; your dream made you feel excited. It energised and motivated you.

SMALL CHANGES

Naturally, I realise it's not always possible – or practical - to go from feeling miserable to joyful in one seamless leap. You're not going to switch from negative to positive thinking overnight but you can start to make small changes to help you feel calmer and reach a more neutral space that will allow you to think more realistically about achieving your goals. You may not have the means to leave your job right now and launch your own business, but you can begin to prepare for that jump. Remember, you don't have to do it all at once. Start by doing some research and see what opportunities are out there. As the American inspirational speaker and author Esther Hicks, known spiritually as Abraham Hicks, memorably says: "You just can't get there from here… you've got to change the way your thoughts are flowing."

Above all, believe in yourself. This is the biggest key to feeling confident and reaching your goals. In today's social media-driven culture, we are constantly being bombarded by influencer images of so-called perfectionism, which only serve to reinforce our feelings about not being "good enough". But have you noticed that those who tend to stand out and rise above the pack are increasingly the ones who are their most authentic selves?

Take Scottish sports commentator Andrew Cotter, who became an Instagram sensation (@mrandrewcotter) in 2020 with his hilarious videos of his two Labradors Olive and Mabel. With his television work having ground to a halt due to the pandemic, he decided to brighten up people's days with clips such as his Grand Final-style commentary of the dogs eating breakfast. He's since become a published author and a Hollywood producer is reportedly interested in his story.

It's a reminder that you never know what can happen when you dare to own your uniqueness and put yourself out there. We all have individual skills and talents and it's about being authentic and believing in ourselves.

When I launched my life coaching clinic in 2007 after finally getting clean, I started by trying to generate some media interest in my business. Each time I spoke to journalists, however, the response was a polite but firm "No thank you". They just weren't interested – not back then anyway! Was I put off? Far from it. Their negativity had nothing to do with whether I could achieve my goal and I wasn't going to let their response affect my confidence. In fact, the more I was rebuffed, the more determined I became to succeed.

I used the 'no's' as rocket fuel to propel me forward because I had a fundamental belief in myself and the business I wanted to create. I had a strong belief that mental health did matter and that people would want to read about how to get better in a magazine or newspaper, so I just believed in myself and my work. I was willing to 'push' in terms of putting in the work and then 'release' – surrendering to the process - to allow my efforts to come to fruition. In that sense, you have to trust that the Universe will support you.

I could write a whole book on my belief in the Universe and our fundamental place in it. I am a deeply spiritual person and I do believe that we are being taken care of, even when it may not appear to be the case. One of my favourite quotes is by the late Native American author and activist Vine Deloria Jr., who stated: "Religion is for people who're afraid of going to Hell. Spirituality is for those who've already been there." That sums me up very well! I strongly believe that if we can work from the inside out; understanding ourselves - our soul and our ego; working on becoming the best we can be, and connecting with something deeper, then our lives really do become blessed and deliver what we need. I also truly believe that when we are brave enough to go for what we want in life – possibly involving a fundamental career change - that the Universe will take care of us and reward us for being true to ourselves. As the American self-help and spiritual author Dr Wayne Dyer once said: "Don't die with your music still in you". That was one of the quotes which really motivated me to become a life coach: I just knew that was what I was here to do, so I went for it. I believe you can, too!

I also actively choose to hold an 'abundance' mindset, whereby I believe there is more than enough for everyone, as opposed to a 'scarcity' mentality, which assumes there will never be enough to go around. I think when people have a scarcity attitude - e.g. "I want to be an interior designer but there are so many out there so why would anyone hire me?" - is the fastest way to being miserable. If you think there is no room for you, there will be no room for you. As I always say, you have to adjust your thoughts....

Some years after I had established my name, I was approached by one particular national newspaper to write an article for their health and wellbeing column. It made me smile when I realised it was the same paper that had turned me down SIX times all those years previously. I have to admit, it was a great moment! I always knew they would ask me one day because I believed strongly enough that they would.

Another experience that could have proved damaging but ended up boosting my confidence, was when I first decided to become a life coach. I contacted an older professional in the same field and he encouraged me to go ahead, so much so that he even suggested I should go into business with him. The prospect of working together encouraged me to study hard and I threw myself into preparing to become a worthy business partner. I remember feeling full of excitement when I arranged to meet him after finishing my studies but unfortunately, the reality was somewhat different. He told me he wanted me to work for him (not with him), taking 80% of my income, and in return, I would be able to use his business name!

Naturally, I politely declined and left the meeting quickly. I remember standing in his office car park afterwards feeling shocked, upset and extremely hurt. I had respected and trusted him but he had merely played on my naivety and inexperience. Even though I felt betrayed and even a little scared, I had no trouble in turning him down because that wasn't what we'd agreed. I thought, "Okay, I will do this on my own then". In hindsight, his attempt to con me was the best thing that could have ever happened to me. It was my first lesson in business and I flew after that.

'BOSS UP'

What we sometimes fail to understand is that setbacks are all part of the journey towards reaching our goals. I love the inspirational meme, "You gonna cry about it or boss up? First of all, imma do both", because it's so human. As I know from personal experience, when you're undergoing recovery for an addiction, it's never a straight line; there are countless curve balls to trip you up and throw you off course along the way. As a society, however, we have this weird rationale that any mishaps or difficulties we encounter are a bad thing. I call this the 'Disneyland attitude'. The problem is, life isn't a Disney movie; things don't always go well for us and nor do we necessarily want them to. Frankly, we need to fail to succeed. Failure is PART of success! Every successful person I know has experienced some kind of failure in their lives and it's those setbacks that have made them resilient and ultimately helped them to get where they are today. As comedian, actor and author Dawn French told The Sunday Times Magazine (18/10/2020): "I like having a go at different things. The desire to keep doing different things is what allows us to make mistakes, it's part of your learning. Sadly, I think we live in a time where mistakes are not forgiven. Everything is the culture of perfection; from body shapes on social media to what's happening with the arts."

We also live in a society that fosters blame; if we don't get the results we think we deserve, then it's often easier to blame others or our circumstances for our misfortune. It's easier to portray ourselves as victims, which allows us to wallow in self-pity. I remember one young client who literally stormed out at the end of our session, complaining that she "didn't feel any better". In that one line, she said it all. She didn't want to do her work or 'believe' that things could get better. She didn't want to help herself to change how she felt, rather, she was happier blaming others for her pain.

Luckily that client did come back about six months later. She was so fed up with being fed up that she was more open to the process, and from that moment, she really started to do her work. She changed a lot during the time we worked together and one year later, sent me an email saying she had been promoted twice. She said she was sure it was due to what she had learnt from me about taking responsibility for her thoughts.

Her experience highlights what I've said repeatedly: it's all about taking responsibility. Don't think for one moment that someone else can 'fix' you, because they can't. People often end up feeling powerless in situations where they have handed over control to someone else, like a boss or a partner. The first thing I ask them is how that makes them feel. If they're being honest, they will admit it makes them feel bad about themselves. Once they realise that they are choosing to feel that way and that they can't blame someone else for their thoughts, they can start to change their mindset and move towards reaching their goals.

Okay, now time to get to work!

CASE STUDY

A few years ago, a very charming young woman came into my office and said she felt overwhelmed and could never reach any goal she set for herself. She didn't believe in herself enough. She had a beautiful family: two young children and a loving husband. From the outside she looked like she had it all but on the 'inside', she felt that she was not confident enough to do what she really wanted - which was to move, with her family, back to her home country. She loved London but, ultimately, in her heart-of-hearts, her goal was to return to the country of her birth. She just didn't know how to actually act on her intention, which was why she came to me for help. Within a few months of working together, she had changed her thoughts enough to start believing in herself and go for her goal – moving home with her family.

Some months later, she sent me her Google review. I was so touched by what she wrote:

"I feel extremely lucky and privileged to have met Jacqueline now and not a minute later! Spending time with her working through my shortcomings is the best investment I ever made. Jacqueline helped me so much after just a few sessions. I am dealing with situations – that would have otherwise been unmanageable for me and would have destroyed me emotionally – in a way that I never thought I was capable of. I am able to calmly and firmly stand up for myself and I am coming out of tough moments stronger, more confident and more empowered than ever. I will be forever

grateful to Jacqueline for guiding me in this beautiful journey of learning how to redirect my thoughts and take control of my emotions which is enabling me to turn my perception of situations around for the better and, in turn, really improving my life. By the way the sessions are SO much fun; it is very uplifting to be around Jacqueline. I cannot wait to continue to work with her and see more results. I highly recommend her, so don't doubt: go see her, spend the time, do the work. You will only regret not having done it earlier!"

WORKSHEET

Ask yourself the following questions

What is the goal I want to achieve?

_____

_____

Why is achieving this goal important to me?

_____

_____

What will my life look like when I have achieved this goal?

_____

_____

What feelings will I have once I have achieved this goal?

_____

_____

How will I benefit from reaching this goal?

_____

_____

What is the first step I need to take to start making this goal a reality?

_____

_____

Who will support me?

_____

_____

Who won't support me?

_____

_____

What are 5 thoughts I can create right now, that can make me feel good and want to take the action so that I can start working towards this goal, ASAP?

_____

_____

_____

_____

_____

CHAPTER EIGHT:

HOW TO BREAK UNHEALTHY HABITS

Do you find yourself caught in a cycle of dieting and bingeing, drinking, shopping, gambling or drug-taking?

As humans, we can quickly fall into unhealthy habits almost without even realising. We may automatically reach for that glass of wine, vial of cocaine or block of chocolate every time something happens in our lives that we think we can't control. And over time, it becomes a bad habit or, worse, an addiction. Of course, we delude ourselves by thinking that it's much easier to drink, take drugs, binge-eat, gamble or have reckless sex than it is to admit we're unhappy with our lives.

We slip into an unconscious way of thinking because it is easier to continue with harmful behaviour than to sit in an uncomfortable new space. We train our brains to avoid our true feelings. We will make excuses for our self-medicating behaviour along the lines of, "I've had a bad day" or "My childhood was terrible", as though our feelings are something removed from us; outside of us. And, therefore, out of our control.

But trust me – for I have been there - it's never really about the destructive habit itself; it's about what is going on inside us that is the key. Our thoughts and feelings are what create our actions and this is what we always need to be mindful of.

The only reason why any of us ever want anything – whether material possessions or illicit substances - is that we believe we will feel better once we have it. But that is just masking the real problem – and no, those things won't make you feel better. The longer you continue with an unhealthy habit, the worse you will usually feel.

I'm here to tell you that *only you* can choose how you feel and that all your feelings are within your control. This does not mean that you cannot or must not feel a negative feeling. Obviously, there are times when it is imperative and human to have a negative feeling. If your beloved dog dies, it would be a little strange if you didn't feel sad or low for a while. It is, of course, important that we actually *feel* our feelings and don't pretend that they don't exist. What I teach, though, is that when you have had enough of feeling utterly fed up/miserable/frustrated (or whatever it is that you are feeling that is heavy and negative), then it is up to you to decide how long you want to remain there – and when you are ready to change how you feel, you do actually have a choice and the power, to fully and completely change your feelings! If you want to feel bad then, of course, you can. But who really wants to feel bad?

Once you understand that it is your thinking that generates your feelings and that you have a choice as to how you think and behave, your life will start to change for the better.

I'm not going to sugar coat it, though. Breaking unhealthy habits or overcoming addictions is hard. Really hard. Because it is our thoughts that create our problems, we've got to develop a strong mind to overcome whatever happens to be our addiction or unhealthy habit of choice. They are the symptoms – cravings for food, sex, alcohol, cigarettes etc – but not the problem, so we need to be willing to look at what is going on in our minds to make us engage in this kind of self-destructive behaviour. If you are drinking excessively, for example, what else is going on in your life to make you feel stressed? What are you trying to ignore and why?

Often, we will use food or alcohol or drugs to numb our feelings, to the point where we don't feel anything anymore. Habits develop as a way of hiding our feelings. You might take up smoking because you are lonely without even realising that is the reason why you smoke, and before you know it, you are addicted. It is much easier to continue to smoke than to confront feelings of loneliness. It's much easier to run away from our problems than to put down that drink or cigarette and face ourselves - and our feelings.

ADMIT YOU'VE GOT A PROBLEM

So, admitting you have a problem is the first step. If a client comes to me and says he can happily down a bottle of wine a night and doesn't think he's got a problem, because, after all, that's what everyone else is doing, then that is fine. He's convinced himself that his alcohol intake is acceptable, normal even, and there is nothing I can do to help him. But what if I asked him to stop drinking for six months? How would he feel? Would he be able to stop? The answer, most likely, is no.

You've got to be ready, willing and able to put in the work required to break a destructive habit or addiction. Often, it's all about timing and that can often mean we might have to hit rock bottom first. The moment you are ready to change is most likely to be the point at which your back is up against the proverbial brick wall. It's when you are ready to let go and surrender as opposed to continuing to push and fight (more on this later). The minute a client tells me they are not okay about their addiction or habit, whether it's drinking a bottle of wine a day or being caught in a cycle of dieting and bingeing, then we can get to work.

How do we build a strong mind? By recognising that we need to change; by choosing the right thoughts and realising that our lives will be much better – and happier – when we do so. As someone who has battled anorexia, bulimia, drugs and alcoholism, I can testify that life is always better on the other side of an addiction. Always.

As American neuroscientist and author Dr Joe Dispenza says: "Your personality creates your personal reality". What he is saying is that our personalities are made up of our thoughts, actions and feelings - and they create our personal reality. I couldn't agree more because it speaks to our capacity as human beings to overcome challenges and change our lives - if we so wish.

Think about his words: "Everything we do, think, feel etc, creates the reality we live in. The first step is awareness. The challenge is that when we change, our subconscious mind (ego) is trying to keep us 'safe' and wants us to revert to familiar habits and behaviours, when in reality, it's just a perceived stress of leaving behind our old identity." The choice to change starts in our minds – we are all capable of change and, therefore, if we are prepared to put in the work, there is nothing stopping us from becoming who we really want to be.

When you, as a person, have a strong personal reality, you are not reliant on or bound by external or artificial things. You are not addicted to anything. The question is, are you willing to push through and overcome your natural resistance to change?

HOW I HIT ROCK BOTTOM

I started my life coaching business in 2007 after dealing with my own addiction battles. I slipped into drugs and alcohol at the highly impressionable age of 15. I was anorexic, bulimic, addicted to exercise, depressed and suffered terrible anxiety and crippling low self-esteem. I simply couldn't handle life. In my mid-20s, after a decade of constant self-abuse, I hit rock bottom and decided something had to change. No matter what it took I was going to transform my life.

So, what did that 'rock bottom' look like for me? Well, it wasn't a pretty sight. I was very, very sick. There were so many times when I should have died from the number of drugs I was taking on a daily basis, and at one point, my anorexia was so bad, I weighed just 40kg.

But it was when I was at my lowest that I was finally able to admit to my mother, that I was an addict and needed help. She and my father vowed to do whatever it took to help me and it was then that my mindset shifted. I was so relieved I could stop the fight with drugs that I was willing to do anything to get clean, sober and healthy. I had to get better because otherwise I would die.

I remember sitting in my first NA meeting (I did the 12-Step recovery programme instead of rehab) with my hoodie up, unable to even say my own name. My nails were broken, my hair had fallen out and I looked and felt a mess but I was determined to get clean. I wanted to stop running away from myself and do the work necessary to change my thinking, and therefore, my life.

That was on 27 August 2003 and, I'm happy to admit, the first year of getting clean was tough. Tougher than anything I had ever experienced before. It was like learning how to live again – learning to eat and sleep properly, learning how to speak again, how to look people in the eye, how to brush my teeth, get properly dressed etc. It was life changing.

Once I started to peel back the layers and get to the root of my problems and actually acknowledge my feelings, I literally felt like I was thawing out. Throughout this time my focus was on getting better, not on the need to score drugs. It was a powerful mindset shift. I realised that spirituality alongside fellowship, and of course, most importantly, challenging my thoughts and beliefs, were the answers to my problems - and if I could get those right, I would get everything else right. I worked the Steps about six times with amazing people helping me along the way, and after six years, I was ready to leave the meetings because I wanted to cross that metaphorical bridge back into the functioning world – to what they call 'normal living'. I felt that I had really torn myself down in order to rebuild myself and I had done so much work, just so much work! I also didn't want to be labelled a recovering alcoholic or drug addict anymore because I felt that labelling myself in that way would keep me small and I knew that life was much bigger than that for me. I wanted to be free to continue my journey of learning and evolving as a person without any limiting labels attached.

I've since studied all over the world and have come across people desperate for advice and guidance - just as I had been years before. They turned to me asking for help. Having been there myself, I found it easy to appreciate the battles they were fighting. More and more people approached me and it became evident my coaching practice had to be set up. It also became very clear that I had gone through what I had gone through for an obvious reason! These days, I grab life with both hands and believe strongly that anything is possible.

One of the most powerful questions I was asked during my recovery was whether I could "pay the bill emotionally" if I started using drugs again. In other words, if I relapsed, would I be able to deal with the emotional fallout? How much worse would I feel? That really hit home. While it's relatively easy to put down the drugs you've been taking and 'get clean', it's another thing to 'stay' clean. In the same way, you can stop smoking but can you remain smoke-free? You can get sober, but staying sober is the hard part. But, of course, it's not hard unless you think it is. Focus on what is going on in your head and think about the consequences if you fall off the wagon etc.

Although my main issue was drugs rather than alcohol, there's no question that I had to be sober in order to get clean. The two go hand-in-hand. But while I'm a big believer that it makes sense for the first few years of your recovery to not drink, I also think you can get to a place where alcohol no longer has any hold over you. In my case, if I feel like a glass of wine, I will have one. The point is, I no longer *need* one to get me through the day. Alcohol no longer holds any power over me; the threat that it once posed to my health and sanity is gone. I have zero desire to do anything that takes me away from myself because I'm happy within myself these days and I'm no longer running away: from any pain or trauma or stress. In contrast, I would never ever go near drugs again; the desire has absolutely disappeared. It actually turns my stomach to think of taking drugs today.

As I touched on previously, in order to succeed in beating any addiction or unhealthy habit, you have to be willing to surrender.

Although there is no conclusive evidence to show that specific personality types are more prone to addiction, it's clear that Type A personalities are more likely to want to 'fight and push' than surrender. This was certainly my experience. As a typical Type A personality, I'm competitive, ambitious and something of a perfectionist, whereas Type B's are more likely to be relaxed and easy-going. Some studies have shown that Type A's lean more towards addiction because we can be harder on ourselves and less forgiving, which means that we'd rather push and fight to maintain control than let go and surrender, which implies giving up.

But actually, if you are battling an addiction, surrendering is exactly what you need to do; it represents a positive step as it shows that you are ready to give up a fight you frankly have no chance of ever winning. Think of your addiction as an internal war – if you accept that the war is over and that you don't have to wake up each morning feeling primed for another day of battle, you will gradually start to feel the weight lift from your shoulders and eventually discover a new-found freedom.

Remember, though, that the road to recovery is not a straight line, so don't beat yourself up if you don't succeed straight away. Set-backs are all part of seeking the final goal and can be what ultimately move you forward.

MY EATING DISORDERS

There's a huge difference between an eating disorder and a drugs problem. You can come off drugs and stay clean with a lot of courage, tenacity and effort. It's very tough but it is possible. Much as conquering my drug addiction was hell for me, my problems with food were far more difficult to overcome because you cannot 'come off' food. You have to eat to live.

This is why anorexia nervosa is considered the most deadly of all mental illnesses – it has the highest mortality rate - and is one of the hardest to treat. An estimated 1.25 million people in the UK have an eating disorder but that figure is considered to be conservative as research in this country is limited. Whereas in the U.S., studies have found that more than 30 million Americans suffer from a clinically significant eating disorder at some stage in their life with approximately six percent of those diagnosed with anorexia likely to die from the disease.

I want to tell you a bit about my experience with eating disorders because, as horrendous as it was, it's also a story of hope and positivity. It's one of the main reasons why I do what I do today, which is to help thousands of people with their eating problems. Every day, I feel grateful I am still alive. There were so many times I should have died from either drugs or starvation.

My body image issues started with a vengeance when I was 15 but it was five years earlier when I first became aware of not feeling good about myself. It was the day of my sister's party, and I was ten years old. I had never thought about how my body looked until I tried on her denim skirt in her bedroom, where she and her friends were hanging out.

The skirt didn't fit me. I remember the disapproving looks and the quiet sniggering from my sister and her friends and thought to myself: "This isn't good."

For the first time in my life, I felt embarrassed and 'less than' and not good enough. I felt like I didn't 'fit in'. I'll never forget that day because it was the moment my body issues started. That skirt had sown a seed of body dissatisfaction in my head because I truly thought: "If I was good enough, I would have fitted into that skirt."

By the time I reached 15, my world was imploding: my parents were often away, I was being bullied at school and struggling to cope. I decided that the only thing I could do was to focus on something I could control - my body and what I ate. Becoming skinny was something to aim for and become 'good at' during a very unhappy phase in my life.

From the age of 15 to 25, I was on a rollercoaster veering between anorexia and bulimia, diet pills and exercise addiction and starvation. The more I tried to control my food intake, the less control I had. I used amphetamines as a way to curb my appetite and stay thin. I did anything I could to control the shape of my body, and somehow, my mixed-up head reached the conclusion that using drugs was fine because as long as I was thin, it was okay.

I had dizzy spells and fainted regularly. I would sit down for dinner with my family and eat one piece of broccoli before calling it a day. Food, or the lack of it, took over my life. My body obsession started affecting other aspects of my life including relationships and my appearance. I had social anxiety and didn't want to eat in front of other people; my hair began to fall out to the point where I had bald patches at the back of my head; I found it difficult to breathe and concentrate, and my fingernails stopped growing. At my lowest point, both mentally and weight-wise, when I tipped the scales at 40kg, the only clothes I could find to fit me were in a children's store, labelled for a seven-year-old girl.

My state of mind and physical health were getting worse but I continued to struggle to control my food intake, consoling myself with the thought that as long as I could do that, I was fine, even though it was messing up my whole life.

At 18, working at an advertising agency, one of my female colleagues gave me a book about anorexia. My immediate reaction was, how dare you! I took it and didn't even say thank you. I threw it straight in the bin. Clearly, she could see how sick I was but I had no idea just how ill I was even though my clothes were falling off me.

There were days when I could barely manage an apple while on other days, I couldn't throw enough sweets and chocolate down my throat. I was all over the place but I had blocked my emotions to the point where I didn't feel anything; I was a non-feeling person.

SEEKING HELP

Eventually I realised that I needed help and booked an appointment at a well-known treatment clinic, where the woman who saw me simply gave me an eating plan. It was frustrating because I didn't need an eating plan, I needed a psychological plan. I tried about 20 different therapists, groups and centres, with most of them telling me I needed a meal plan and should write down everything I ate each day. Meal plans are not the answer when you have an overwhelming fear of putting on weight. Being reminded of what you are consuming is not even remotely helpful. It simply made me want to control what I ate even more.

I knew that if I was going to get well I had to eat but I was in a lot of emotional pain as I started to put on weight. I ate and I ate and I ate…my body was rebelling against the years of starvation and I was living my worst nightmare. I had finally managed to give up control but it was the worst thing I could have done to myself. I couldn't stop myself from thinking controlling thoughts, and while I knew I could restrict again if I chose to, how was I going to get better if I did that? I just couldn't diet any more. I couldn't take one more day of restricting.

I became even more desperate to get help as I just wanted to get better and stop fighting this exhausting body image and weight problem that had indoctrinated my brain and taken over my entire life.

It took a long time for me to finally surrender and stop hating myself. My body eventually balanced itself out from the starvation, bingeing, restriction and diet cycle when I finally gave up the fight and instead, became resigned to this just being how it was.

In a strange way, feeling resigned was the start of my journey of self-discovery. I began to understand myself better. It took time and effort but I learned to become willing to face my fears, to understand why I thought I needed to do this to myself, and then by accident (except I don't believe in accidents), halfway through getting better mentally but when I was at my heaviest, I stumbled across a woman in New York who was to be a saviour in my recovery. She was a tough-talker like me and had been on exactly the same journey as I had with drugs, food issues, bingeing and starvation. She just got it. We had a great connection; she understood me from the start and her wise words and advice helped me though the first chapter of my recovery.

I had already started studying emotional eating in a bid to work out why I was making these destructive choices, and as I began to understand myself better, this therapist helped me to take the next step and choose a new path. She made me aware that if lived somewhere in Africa, where it's considered beautiful to be a size 22, I wouldn't have a problem with body image. She also taught me that this issue was far bigger than me: it was about the patriarchal society and the myth that we needed to look a certain way in order to be socially acceptable.

I realised that I had to stop rebelling against my body and start rebelling instead against society, stick two fingers up and say: I'm not fitting into your standards anymore.". From feeling resigned, I suddenly felt as if I had won the lottery. I started to understand what had happened on a deeper level and I was now free. Knowledge is power and it was beautiful.

I learned it was important to get rid of my scales and stop measuring my self-worth by my weight. I had to accept that being thin didn't make me happy and that I'd been controlling my food intake as a way to deal with – or avoid – my feelings.

The day I made the decision to stop dieting and embrace 'allowance', I went into a café in London and bought myself a chocolate almond croissant. I sat down and took my time to enjoy eating it; to eat consciously. Once you make the choice to stop dieting and allow yourself to eat, you realise that it's not about choosing which types of food make up the perfect existence. That is a diet mentality. Everything ebbs and flows.

It took time for me to learn to trust myself again but I was willing to do whatever it took. At first, I didn't stop eating because I could, but then, weirdly, I quickly got fed up with being able to have pizza for breakfast, lunch and dinner, and I gradually started to change my approach to food.

After about a month of eating whatever I wanted without restriction, someone came to my apartment with some chocolate brownies for tea and I genuinely didn't want one. I thought, "Oh my God, can this be true? Have I just turned away brownies, truly knowing I didn't want them?" I was in awe! I actually had a moment where I paused between being offered the brownie, giving myself an option and then deciding, "Actually, no, I don't feel like it, thanks.". I was in a completely different mental space and I can't tell you how empowering and liberating that felt.

It's an evolution of removing the layers and learning how to be kind to yourself. Today, I still rebel (of course) but it's in a self-loving and non-punishing way. I rebel against society by choosing to like myself and by not giving a hoot what shape my body is because it doesn't 'mean' anything. I rebel against society because it's not up to anyone else to tell me if I'm good enough. I eat what I want to eat and I am guided by my body. I trust it. I don't want to be in that sad and lonely place, feeling that pain, ever again.

DIETS DON'T WORK

I have some momentous news to break to you. Diets are designed to fail. You are not meant to succeed on a diet because it is a multi-million-pound industry and it wants you to keep coming back for more. Diets are set up for you to never ever win the 'weight battle'. That's the whole point. If diets worked, you would never have to do them more than once. If the last diet you had bought or followed was a success, you'd do it once, achieve your goal weight and that would be the end of it. And you wouldn't be reading this book. Right?

Let's analyse exactly what a diet is. A diet is considered to be anything that makes you restrict food in any shape or form. It's not rocket science. That's it. And it relates to any diet known to man. Any way in which you are trying to control your food by depriving yourself is a diet but unless you are medically unable to eat certain types of food, you should not be restricting your food or choices.

Diets are fundamentally based on controlling your food intake but the ability to control what you eat each day is a myth in itself. Why, you may ask? It's quite simple. You can't control your food intake in the same way that you can't control your body temperature or your height, for that matter. Trying to control your food is a bit like going for a run but asking yourself to make sure you don't sweat. You simply can't do that! It's a complete impossibility, just like the idea that we can control our food consumption.

Now ask yourself this. If you don't have a problem with your body, why would you want to control what you eat anyway?

You might have guessed by now that I don't believe in diets. Let me explain why. The diet cycle starts with what I call wagon thinking. You say to yourself: "I need to go on a diet. I'm going to be good today, I'm going to be healthy and cut back."

So, you start the day in a puritanical fashion with yoghurt and fruit, then you eat a salad at lunchtime. So far, so saintly. Then, at 4pm, when someone brings a beautiful cake into the office for their birthday or your children come home with the cookies they made at school, the demon on your shoulder tells you to 'get stuck in'. But you shouldn't, but you want to, but you mustn't and inevitably, you fall off the so-called 'wagon'. This is all quite normal by the way because – I'll say it again – you can't control your food intake.

You're off the wagon and then you feel down; a failure. You say: "Great, I've ruined my diet already so I might as well continue eating all this 'bad' stuff today because I can always start the diet again tomorrow." Suddenly, you have scooted from 'being good' to bingeing like there is no tomorrow because that mischievous little voice in your head is telling you, "I CAN NEVER EAT THAT FOOD AGAIN!". The brain flips off into: "Oh, my God, I'd better have it all now then", and the next morning, the whole damn cycle starts over again.

Once again, the myth that you will "start the diet again tomorrow" is one of the main reasons you stay stuck in wagon thinking. As if being on the wagon is the safest thing for you to do, some holy grail that will get you to where you want to be in life via your body shape. Your brain trills: "If that wagon is there I will be okay", except going on and off the wagon, or diet, *is the problem.*

Once I explain this to my clients, they understand, nod their heads in agreement and then look at me with abject fear in their eyes. They hit a point where they are terrified. They start to understand the wagon is the problem...BUT NOW WHAT? This is a place of fear, it's where the terror comes in, and they start thinking: "But if I haven't got a diet to fall back on, what am I going to do?"

I'm guessing this is all sounding rather familiar. But the good news is, you have already taken the first step towards undoing years, possibly decades, of this kind of negative thinking (which you may not have even been aware of as it's often sub-conscious). The first thing I want to explain is why you have to rebel against that way of thinking. The wagon is not your saviour, it is not your best friend, it is actually your enemy. If you really want to change things, you are going to have to learn how to eat all over again. Effectively, think of it as retraining yourself.

WEIGHT-OBSESSED CULTURE

The way I have helped lots of people with their emotional eating problems may seem counterintuitive, but trust me it works. In order to change your emotional eating pattern, you need to start to allow *all* foods. It takes baby steps to retrain your brain but after a while, you will find that food no longer holds the same power over you.

Let's think about how a child eats. When you are young, you are not even aware of this but you somehow know exactly when you are hungry and when you are full. You don't need a book or a points system to tell you that. We seem to think we have lost that instinct but actually, we haven't. It's still there and we have to take ourselves back to that place again, as a child, where we can trust ourselves once again.

We were born with hunger and the only thing diets do is to disconnect us from that very basic and fundamental human instinct. We choose to trust a diet sheet to tell us what we need rather than listening to our instincts. Now isn't that the most dysfunctional thing ever? I mean, how exactly does a diet sheet know what our bodies need? The only person who knows what you need is YOU. Diets are the cause of the problem not the answer.

Of course, diets don't exist in a vacuum.

We live in a society where we are constantly bombarded with unrealistic images and photographs of women that have been photoshopped or doctored, which is unhelpful if your body image isn't strong or confident. Magazines, newspapers, television and social media all continue to present an idealised image of what our body shape should be, reinforcing this with "bikini ready" summer diets, applauding celebrities who lose weight – when singer Adele lost weight, the media described it as an "amazing physical transformation" – and generally brainwashing people into believing that to be 'worthy', you have to be a certain size.

We live in a weight-obsessed culture where people feel it's okay to comment on your size and shape; to judge the way you look. But, actually, it isn't. Your body is unique to you and no two bodies are the same, so trying to define your worth by your size is completely pointless and potentially harmful. You are more than the shape of your body.

Fortunately, the tide is slowly starting to turn and the worldwide body positivity movement is helping to change people's attitudes and perceptions, especially on social media.

Campaigners like Ashley Graham, Tess Holliday and Jada Sezer, and influencers such as my client and now friend Emily Clarkson, have amassed hundreds of thousands of followers by pushing back against society's diktats and showing that the number on the scale or the size of your jeans do not determine your self-worth or define who you are. Glossy magazines are also beginning to celebrate more diverse body shapes and sizes, with, for example, singer Lizzo featured on the cover of American Vogue magazine's October 2020 issue.

If you want to change your relationship with the way you eat, you have to understand that shifting a negative body image is critical to changing your attitudes around food. You cannot change your behaviour to food if you don't like your body. You have to learn how to love your body first and foremost. We weren't born with negative body thoughts; they've been imposed on us by society, so we need to break free from this tyranny. And remember, loving your body can simply start with acceptance.

Only you have the power to change your thoughts and stop running away from whatever has been causing your emotional blockages. Once you reach the point of self-acceptance, that is where the magic begins.

CASE STUDY

When I first met a young female client working in the City, her food issues were at an all-time high and her body image at an all-time low. Her job was demanding and her life was hectic and her diet was pretty much all over the place. She hated her body and struggled with what to eat and when. She dieted and restricted, she binged and purged. She even got to the point of not filling up her fridge because she was scared she would just eat all of it in one go. If she ate so much as a dessert at a restaurant she would berate herself. This started affecting her social life to the point where she would turn down plans to see her friends so she didn't have to eat. She was in a seriously bad place when she finally walked into my office. We worked together over a period of two months to help her unravel all of her conflicting thoughts about eating and dieting and got to the stage where she was able to step into allowance: she went from making so many food types off-limits and 'not allowed', to 'allowing' all foods, which required bravery and courage. She realised that letting go was the healing she ultimately needed and her life literally did a 180.

This was the review she left me:

"When I first met Jacqueline I was a neurotic, food mess. I had spent as much of my life as I can remember obsessing about food - morning, noon and night. To say obsessing about food and body image dominated my life really is not an understatement. I turned to Jacqueline for help and together we cracked it and my life has completely changed. I

have gone from someone who NEVER had any food in the fridge to a person that can comfortably go food shopping and know I won't spend days bingeing, purging and then hating myself. Mentally berating my body constantly in front of the mirror has stopped and I have so much more time and energy to spend on things far more worthwhile. It's a pretty tough journey but utterly worthwhile. PS: Jacqueline, I'm in a cafe and I cried writing that!"

WORKSHEET

Choosing to Quit the Game

Sit down somewhere quiet and ask yourself the following questions. Write down the answers as honestly as you can

How many diets have you tried?

_____

_____

How many years of your life have you spent on a diet?

_____

_____

Were you happy in your life (not your body) the last time you were thin?

_____

_____

What has made you pick up this book now?

_____

_____

What would you like to accomplish with this process?

_____

_____

Are you ready to start this journey towards changing your life for the better?

_____

_____

How do you think your life will change when you are at peace with food and your body? What are you willing to do to achieve this?

_____

_____

_____

_____

On a scale of 1 to 10, how important is it for you to find peace with food and your body?

_____

_____

If you are not ready now, when do you think you will be?

_____

_____

This is your starting point for change and it will be useful to look back on as you continue this journey and see how far you have come.

Supporting the child in you:

Think back to the very first time you were made to feel ashamed about your body shape or size.

Who influenced you or taught you about your body at a young age?

___

What was their view on body image?

___

How old were you?

___

Was it a throwaway comment or was it aimed at you?

___

How did that make you feel?

_____

_____

Can you pinpoint it as the start of your journey into a body-obsessed state of mind?

_____

_____

Could it be possible that the person making that comment had also been conditioned into a certain way of thinking about body image?

_____

_____

If you could speak to the five-year-old you or the eight-year-old you on that day now, what would you say to them? Write a short letter to your younger self, using your experience and the benefit of hindsight, and write down what you would say to your younger self.

_____

_____

_____

_____

CHAPTER NINE:

HOW TO IMPROVE ALL YOUR RELATIONSHIPS

Do you want to avoid pitfalls and establish better, more fulfilling relationships?

Life is about relationships.

One of the most important things in most of our lives is our relationships with others. These can be relationships with bosses, work colleagues, friends, family or romantic partners.

As an ultra-social species, human beings are wired to crave belonging; to feel part of a close-knit tribe, whether in the home, workplace, neighbourhood or wider community. On every level – neurological, biological and psychological - we tend to function better when we're surrounded by and connected to others. As countless studies have shown, lack of human company or social support can lead to long-term physical and mental problems. For instance, people who are lonely are more prone to chronic stress and depression, which can even increase the risk of cardiovascular disease and cancer and cause reduced immune function.

Conversely, people who are socially connected are more likely to be happier and healthier -and their brains actually perform better, too. Studies have also revealed that those in satisfying relationships tend to live longer, with some reports suggesting that stronger social ties increase the likelihood of an individual's overall survival by as much as 50 percent.

The key here is good or satisfying relationships. A long-running Harvard Medical School study of adult development analysed the health of more than 700 men over their lifetime, starting in 1938. It found that people in the study who were most satisfied in their relationships at the age of 50 were also the healthiest at 80. The Harvard Study of Adult Development director Dr Robert Waldinger explained: "Our most happily partnered men and women reported in their 80s that on days when they had more physical pain, their mood stayed just as happy." He also noted: "Being in a securely attached relationship is protective in your 80s. Those people's memories stay sharper longer. People who feel they can't count on the other person, experience early memory decline. Living in conflict, such as in a high-conflict marriage, is bad for your health."

That is a big statement right there. And proof that living in high conflict relationships is bad for our health. This is something I absolutely know from first-hand experience to be true.

So, the quality of our relationships is what matters most but how many of us can claim to have happy, fulfilled and balanced relationships? As innate as our need to belong is, it's also a very human trait to struggle with our friendships, platonic or otherwise: you only have to glance at any agony aunt column to see that one of the most common issues is relationship woes.

Two of the most important communication skills you can have in terms of building and maintaining solid relationships are rapport and listening.

BUILDING RAPPORT

Rapport is the ability to understand and communicate with others in a harmonious and empathetic way and is key to forging long-lasting relationships. It is imperative when building any form of relationship, either with individuals or groups, that rapport is used in a way that makes communication possible or easy. Good rapport helps build great relationships. It is a necessity. It connects you with others so that both parties feel comfortable, relaxed and readily open, which means you can build the relationship from a place of trust.

Rapport is the most important characteristic of unconscious human interaction and can sometimes happen naturally. Instinctively, you will know when you are 'in sync' with someone or on the same 'wavelength', meaning that you understand them from the start. But you can also build rapport consciously by finding common ground through shared experiences and views, including a shared sense of humour, and by being empathetic.

It's essential to put time and effort into developing rapport because of the benefits it can bring to you both personally and professionally – employers are more likely to hire someone who they believe will fit in with their existing team and personal relationships will be smoother if there is an emotional connection.

So, how do you build rapport? The first thing to know is that you are the message and all parts of you need to be working in harmony. For example, if you don't look confident - as if you don't believe in your message - then people are less likely to listen to what you are saying.

How you look, how you sound and what you say determine how communication is received and responded to. A University of California study found that 55 percent of communication is conveyed through gestures, expression and posture; 38 percent through the quality/tone of your voice, and seven percent through your words. Therefore, the perception of your sincerity comes not so much from what you say but how you say it and how you show an appreciation for and understanding of the other person's thoughts and feelings.

Clearly, first impressions count so it's imperative that you understand rapport and communication when building relationships with others.

Communication is so important – and just as key is comprehension! Communicating with someone is one thing, making sure there is comprehension of what you are communicating is quite another.

One of the most effective Neuro Linguistic Programming (NLP) techniques for building rapport and helping you to communicate is matching and mirroring, whereby you match and mirror the other person's body language and other non-verbal signals. You only have to watch two friends talking to see how they sub-consciously mimic each other's non-verbal communication. Try to maintain eye contact for at least 60% of the time but not so much as to make the other person feel uncomfortable; match your body language with theirs, including how they are sitting or standing; adjust your breathing rhythm to theirs, which unconsciously shows that you are in sync, and try to keep the same pitch and pace in terms of tone and tempo of your voice. Open body language is also an ice-breaker. If you lean towards the person you are talking to with your hands open and your arms and legs uncrossed, then this will help both of you to feel more relaxed. The other person will automatically believe your body language over what you are saying, so it's important to appear as open and relaxed as possible.

It's also useful to reflect back and clarify what the other person has said by repeating their words, as this shows you've not only been listening but helps to establish common ground by using their words and phrases. You don't have to like or agree with their viewpoint but it helps to be open-minded and try to understand it. Looking at the world from someone else's perspective can be an effective way to resolve conflict and help you reach a clearer understanding and resolution. When you are in rapport, you can disagree with what someone says but still relate respectfully to them.

LEARN HOW TO *REALLY* LISTEN

We have conversations with people all the time – our friends, family, colleagues and loved ones - but how well do we really listen?

Listening can have a big impact on the quality of our relationships with others, yet research suggests that we only remember between 25 and 50 percent of what we hear and that we simply do not absorb the whole message that others attempt to convey to us.

A lot of the time we confuse listening with "waiting to reply with an answer". We often speak over people or try to get our point across while someone else is talking, which sends a signal that we believe what we have to say is more important than what they're trying to say. This is not a good start if you want to build strong relationships.

I'm happy to admit that becoming a life coach changed my perception of listening. After studying hard for some years, I asked an older, more experienced therapist friend if he would give me one piece of advice to become the best coach I could be. "Jacqueline, when your clients talk, you have to SHUT THE F…. UP AND LISTEN or you miss the gold," he told me. That was great advice and something I will never forget. From that day on, I never looked back and now, when people start to talk, I really listen. It took time to learn how to shut up and listen properly as it's a skill that must be learned, but once I did, it unlocked everything for me - because when you truly listen, you hear what people say, not what you think they say.

There are so many advantages to being a good or better listener - you will improve not only your productivity and knowledge, but your relationships too, and you will also increase your ability to negotiate, influence and understand others. Learning to listen also gives you the ability to avoid conflict and misunderstandings.

So, how do we improve our listening skills? The fastest way to do this is to become tuned into what is called 'conscious listening', whereby you make a concentrated and mindful effort to hear the words that the other person is saying, and at the same time, try to understand the complete message being sent. In other words, you are not thinking about what you want to say in return while they are talking. Instead, you are listening to them.

You can show the person speaking to you that they have your undivided attention by looking directly at them; by not letting anything else distract you; by using your body language to show you are paying attention, and by using the person's name as often as you can (the latter being a great tip from the brilliant writer and self-improvement pioneer Dale Carnegie). Don't interrupt with counter-arguments while they are still speaking. You can offer your opinion/feedback once they have finished.

Above all, conscious listening is about respect and understanding in a non-judgmental way.

It's really important to work on the following sentence: that just because you may not agree with the other person, it doesn't mean they are 'wrong'; they may simply hold a different opinion to you. Try to be open, calm and honest in your response and treat the other person in the same way you would wish to be treated. Conscious listening is your secret weapon in your rapport-building armoury and once you have practised these skills, you will very quickly see how your relationships and ultimately, your life, will change for the better.

TAKE RESPONSIBILITY

Another critical step towards establishing healthy relationships is to first manage the most important and longest relationship of your life - with yourself!

We can't expect to relate to others if we lack insight into our own thoughts and behaviour. Key to this is taking responsibility for our own actions – and that means we need to stop blaming others for how we feel. We can often be quick to blame our friends, colleagues or loved ones and point out what's wrong with them to deflect blame from ourselves. It could be that we're the ones guilty of toxic behaviour, which is hurting those closest to us. Again, it's about being respectful and understanding and taking the time to find out why they feel the way they do and then trying to take responsibility for our own emotions and make changes where possible.

We must learn to look at our 'part' in situations if we really want to elevate our self and grow.

We all have what I call a 'manual' for other people, namely a handbook of how we believe everyone else should behave and think. But just because we may operate in a certain way, it doesn't mean everyone else should follow suit. For example, if you're invited to a friend's house for dinner and take them a bunch of flowers, but are miffed when they come to your place and don't reciprocate, you are imposing your set of rules which don't necessarily apply to them. This is bound to cause you - and only you - unnecessary hurt, misunderstanding and disappointment. Ultimately, wanting them to behave in the same way as you, is what is creating your pain.

It's all about growing into emotional adulthood and being brave enough to look inwards and check your own thoughts. In other words, how you think creates how you feel; it is never about the other person. That is really hard for people to understand at first but the more we understand and accept this, the easier our lives will become.

I always say, you can't change or control other people. No matter how much we wish someone would act differently, it has to be their choice. They'll only decide to change if they think there's sufficient incentive, such as a happier, more balanced life. But trying to make other people change is a total waste of time and energy.

You may think that if they change, you will feel better but actually, this is not the case. It is about changing your thoughts, in order to feel better – not the other person.

Focus on getting your own mindset right. When people come to me and say they want to get a divorce, I ask them to do nothing until we have closely examined their thoughts first.

The worst thing you can do is to quit a relationship or marriage when you're full of hate or anger. You need to be in a calm and peaceful space before you can make a rational decision about whether to stay or leave. It might seem easy to point the finger at the other person but you have to ask yourself, "What is my part in this? What have I accepted or allowed to happen? Could I have been kinder, more tolerant or more loving?". A relationship enables us to hold a mirror up to ourselves and we can learn a lot in the process – as long as we are willing to put in the effort.

In order to grow, we have to recognise that how we view relationships is influenced by what we learn in childhood. As we've already established, our outlook on life is shaped by our early experiences and social conditioning; we assume the beliefs and opinions of those closest to us and use them as a template for our own interactions. This means that we approach relationships from a subjective and often self-limiting perspective. We may gravitate towards toxic partnerships because of deep-rooted insecurities and lack of self-esteem or self-worth. So, the only way to change or remedy that is to work on ourselves, knowing that if we have high self-esteem, we're going to develop different, more positive relationships.

BELIEF SYSTEMS

A lot of what we learn about love is absorbed when we are young. If we had absent parents, we learn that love is unavailable and usually end up going for unavailable partners as adults. If our parents were overbearing, we learn that love is all consuming and stifling and then we look for that in our adult relationships. What we learnt during our formative years is what influences how we continue to think and act as adults until, of course, we hit a wall and need to unlearn.

This is not to say, though, that your parents have directly 'done this' to you. Rather, it is what you have created in your mind; it is what you have read into something that it might not mean. For example, if you're five years old and your mum comes home tired and fed up after a hard day at work and takes no notice of a picture you've drawn for her, you will automatically assume that it must be your fault she isn't interested. She never actually said that, but this is the explanation you have created in your mind – you have made this situation mean something it didn't mean. And then you carry this thinking with you throughout your adulthood, which is why 'thought' work is so important!

You see, once you are willing to examine your own belief system and acknowledge what you have learnt about relationships, then you will be open to changing your life. When we look at unlearning what we have learnt about love and relationships, we might realise that how we are currently thinking and therefore attracting, doesn't work anymore.

You may even gain the courage to leave a destructive relationship.

For a long time, I dated unavailable men. I became an expert at finding men who were emotionally unavailable to me – all because of what I learnt as a child. I know now that my parents loved me dearly but because they were often abroad while I was growing up, I associated love with being unavailable. In my early 20s, I dated someone whom I thought was the love of my life: he was funny, successful – and married. He had promised to leave his wife, so I gave him one year, and on the last day, he admitted he couldn't go through with it, and broke my heart. It was one of the biggest lessons I learnt because what was I doing going out with a married man in the first place and what did it say about my own self-esteem? I would never allow myself to get myself into a situation like that again but, ultimately, he was a coward and I had a lucky escape.

Unfortunately, that experience didn't stop me from continuing to date the same kind of emotionally detached, commitment-phobic man. Let me tell you, I've suffered some serious heartbreak in my life. It took a lot of failed relationships and a lot of work and therapy to understand why I was attracted to a certain type of man. I had to unlearn much of what I had learnt about the love as a child. I had to relearn what love is as an adult. First and foremost, I had to learn how to fully and completely love and value myself - and do this before I could even think about finding the right relationship. Identifying that unconscious pattern of thinking, changed everything for me - I started dating *available* men, which was a much scarier prospect but something I needed to learn how to do. I'm definitely in a place now where I know myself a lot better and no longer put up with behaviour that I once thought was acceptable. This has opened me up to meeting some different, better and really lovely people. We all have to be aware of our own triggers. For me, it took plenty of hard work, but the journey has been 1000 percent worth it!

Low self-esteem is often at the heart of an imbalanced relationship. I remember one client who came to me in tears because his girlfriend showed him zero respect. She would go out at night and not come home; she flaunted her friendships with other men, even though she knew it made him unhappy, and she continually belittled him. The first thing I told him was to stop trying to understand her behaviour and look, instead, at why he was letting this be okay for him. It had nothing to do with her. It had *everything* to do with him. Once he started to write down all his negative thoughts, he understood that he was allowing himself to be undermined and what he really wanted was a caring relationship based on mutual respect, openness and honesty. Realising that his girlfriend was never going to change and that he had been enabling her behaviour, he found the courage to leave her and shortly afterwards met someone else and they've since had a baby together. He has never felt happier!

It was his lack of self-esteem that kept him prisoner in the relationship.

Let's take a closer look at what the term 'self-esteem' means. It refers to how we view ourselves internally. It's the overall opinion we hold about ourselves and the value we place on ourselves as people. When we have low self-esteem, we think negative thoughts, such as "I'm unlovable" or "I'm useless" or "I'm worthless". Of course, most of us have mixed opinions of ourselves, but if your overall view is that you are inadequate or inferior, or if you believe that you have no true worth and are not entitled to the good things in life – that you are "undeserving" – then this means your self-esteem is fundamentally low.

As this belief is based on your thought process rather than fact, it is really important to gather all the thoughts you hold about yourself that are negative and then start to look for evidence to prove that the opposite is true. For example, if you believe that you are not "lovable", instead of finding evidence to prove this thought is true, you need to start looking for evidence to prove the opposite. You could ask yourself instead, "Who does love me?" – and you will be able to say, "My mum, my dad, my friends, my family, my partner" etc. It becomes hard to believe a thought when you have evidence to prove the opposite is actually true. Thoughts create feelings, therefore positive thoughts create positive feelings!

Tell yourself kind, loving statements that you would say to someone you hold dear. Imagine your best friend talking about you as a person – they would say complimentary things like, "She's funny, kind, thoughtful" etc. When you start looking at yourself from a friend's point of view, you will be amazed at how good you really are. Once you have managed to shift your own perspective, it will help you to see your partner, friend or workmate in a more positive light, too, and you'll inevitably feel better about that relationship. Alternatively, you might realise that you've outgrown that person and are ready to move on, which is equally okay.

I always like to say that rejection is redirection. When someone walks away from you, it's because they are not meant to be in your life. See it as a gift – possibly an unexpected one but no less valuable for the lesson it represents. If someone really doesn't want to be in your life, then what is appealing about that? Why would you try to hold on to such a one-sided relationship? And what is wrong with your sense of self-worth if you do?

RECOGNISING TOXICITY

We often don't even realise just how toxic a relationship is until it's over – or, more specifically, how toxic the other person is!

Let's look at an extreme form of toxicity involving the classic sociopath. There are so many clues that should alert us to sociopathic behaviour but because we have not been educated to understand these personality disorders, it can be very confusing. Unfortunately, it is usually at the end of such relationships that people find out just what they have been dealing with.

It can be very difficult to break free from a sociopath. They are controlling, extremely clever and manipulative: they will criticise you endlessly, ridicule and humiliate you, lie to you, dominate you, and even physically abuse you. They have no intention of ever changing and yet, they are able to reel you in and fool you, because they can also be extremely charming and convincing. They play a game of 'pull you in/spit you out/pull you in/spit you out', which is known as 'trauma bonding'. They gaslight and confuse you for their own perverse pleasure - I know about this, because I was once in a relationship with one. It was truly one of the worst times in my life, like being caught in a Venus Fly trap.

He was charming, good-looking, confident and intelligent and I was mesmerised by his love-bombing (stage one of all sociopathic tactics). But it wasn't long before I found myself being systematically undermined and manipulated. I shouldn't have endured the constant put-downs and bad moods, but I kept falling for his excuses; that he was stressed or tired or drunk, as that's what sociopaths excel at doing. They are pathological liars and they get away with their deceit through sheer force of their own sense of superiority and entitlement. They are experts at masking their behaviour behind a veneer of charm; presenting one face in public and another in private.

As a strong, independent woman, you may wonder why I didn't see the signs straight away? It was the drip-drip effect of his behaviour that caught me off guard (stage two is called the devaluation stage); I was well and truly hooked before I realised what was going on. Interestingly, sociopaths or narcissists tend to target people just like me who are strong, full of life and positivity. They want to squash our joy and enthusiasm and make us question our own reality as a way of exercising control. Watching the other person truly suffer makes them, ultimately, feel better about themselves. They are really very mentally ill.

When that relationship ended, I didn't know what had hit me. I was diagnosed with PTSD and I was pretty much traumatised. I had to do a lot of work on myself to get my mind back to normal after years of gaslighting and confusion, coercive control and consistently having to walk on eggshells. As I didn't want to be labelled or forced to remain stuck in the past, I knew I had to up my game and make myself better. I happened to find a brilliant book by American author and abuse survivor Jackson MacKenzie called Psychopath Free, and suddenly, reading that book, it all made sense. There are 30 pointers at the start to determine if you have, in fact, been in a relationship with a sociopath. My ex had all 30 traits and it sent a shiver down my spine. The more I researched and the more I spoke to others who had endured similar relationship experiences with narcissists, sociopaths and psychopaths, the more I started to talk about it - I could have earned a PhD in the subject! It was a tough experience but I certainly learnt a lot about myself in the process. It changed everything for me and my subsequent relationships. It has been years since that relationship ended, but honestly, my relief is still palpable.

There is a lot to say on this subject but most importantly, the only way to diminish the power of a sociopath is to starve them of fuel; you have to stop giving them opportunities to wrong foot you. For example, if your boss is sociopathic, offer him or her as little personal information as possible because anything you do tell them, will almost certainly be used against you - and at a time designed to deliberately cause you maximum hurt or humiliation.

MUTUAL RESPECT

Sometimes, we forget that relationships don't have to be perfect and that it's normal to have to put the effort in to make them work. We all get a little side-tracked at times by the Hollywood version of love, and believe that once we're whisked off our feet by a handsome prince, then we've got our fairy-tale ending. Job done. But, of course, it doesn't work like that in real life. Relationships can be messy and challenging and they only really work when there's mutual respect and honesty and, most importantly, two-way communication. But it is imperative that you have respect for yourself first.

Everyone's love language is different: it can mean cooking a delicious meal for someone or expressing your feelings through words, such as saying, "I love you". The main thing is that you feel loved – and the effort is equal.

Here's what the Hollywood actress Nicole Kidman has to say about her love for her husband, country music star Keith Urban. By all accounts, the couple have been happily married for 14 years but their relationship could have foundered soon after their wedding in 2006 due to his ongoing drug and alcohol addictions. As he has said, "I caused the implosion of my fresh marriage." She stood by him when he went to rehab that same year and he has since credited her with helping him to become a different man. In an interview with UK Glamour magazine (November 2020), Nicole paid tribute to her husband, saying: "I have a very good relationship...He's a very strong, warm, kind man. I'm very fortunate to have that in my life, because it's a really strong place to be able to go and curl up."

They clearly know what makes each other tick and choose to grow together, fully aware and respectful of their respective vulnerabilities and insecurities.

As Harvard's Dr Waldinger explains, it's important to nurture or improve existing relationships with friends, family or spouses. "People who work on their relationships and stay in healthy relationships are happier," he told Harvard Health Publishing. "It doesn't have to be smooth all the time, as long as you feel you can count on the other when the going gets tough."

Enduring friendships are particularly important – one of the most beneficial things for our mental health is having a strong group of friends around us. I've got four best girlfriends who have been there for me through thick and thin. We talk about everything and they are not afraid to call me out, but I know they've always got my back – and I've got theirs - whatever the situation.

We learn a lot from others and fall into similar habits as the people we socialise with the most. This is why it's so important for us to keep close those who are positive forces in our lives and who love us for who we are. Whereas those who don't really care and are friends out of convenience, can drain us or drag us down and are, ultimately, bad for our mental health.

Don't think of having close relationships as a chore; think of them as part of self-care. As Dr Waldinger said: "Staying connected and involved is actually a form of taking care of yourself, just like exercise or eating right. This is an important prescription for health."

Remember, you are never really alone and you are more loved than you may think you are. It might not feel like it but there is always someone there to offer love, kindness and support. You just need to be willing to reach out and ask for what you need. Letting go may mean showing your vulnerability but that could be just what is required. Ask for love and you will be amazed to discover where you can find it.

CASE STUDY

I had a client come and see me who struggled to maintain relationships with pretty much everyone in her close family. She felt very stuck and hadn't seen them in years but missed them and wanted to reach out, visit them again and just do things differently. When we first started working together, she blamed each and every one of them for how she felt, which, of course, is why she was in such a pickle in the first place. We worked together on her thinking, what she had learnt about love, as well as her 'manual for others'. We discussed how her thoughts were creating her feelings, not her family members, and I taught her how to get her power back through her mindset. She was really down a rabbit hole at first blaming her sisters for most things that had gone wrong in her life and couldn't believe that it wasn't their fault. But the more work we did together, the lighter it all became for her and slowly she empowered herself and was able to put the tools and techniques I had taught her, into action.

A few months later, she sent me this email: "Hi Jacqueline, after our work together I reached out to my family again and we even decided to go to Spain together for a break! I had a lovely time with them and I am so happy that I did the work with you. I can tell just how much I have changed for the better in my everyday life and being with my family was great. I felt very comfortable setting boundaries with them and can now look at my relationships with them objectively. It is such a relief to know that I decide who I am and don't have to be influenced by my past. I cannot thank you enough

WORKSHEET – The Manual for Others:

Make a list of your 'manual' for others.

Below are some examples but you can choose any you want.

Once you have done this, challenge yourself to think differently about these guidelines and see what you can change to start to feel better about yourself – and improve your relationships in the process.

It could be something like, "My friend should call me every day" to something like, "Her not calling me doesn't mean she doesn't love me, she is allowed to be busy as well."

Remember, you wouldn't want someone else telling you what to do, how to think or behave, so don't try to impose your 'guidelines' or rules on them.

YOUR MOTHER (example)

1. She should call me every day to see how I am
2. She shouldn't give my sister more than she gives me
3. She shouldn't wear things I tell her look daft

Now list your manual for

a) Your sibling

b) Your best friend

c) Your boss

_____
_____
_____
_____
_____
_____
_____
_____
_____
_____

CHAPTER TEN

HOW TO BE A SUCCESS

Do you want to learn how to be successful? You already are...but just don't realise it yet!

What does success look like? If we are to believe what we see in the media, we need to be able to tick the following criteria to be considered successful: wealthy, powerful, beautiful, have a husband/wife/partner, four children, and almost always, be famous.

In other words, we are told that the way to measure success is to look at the things we can acquire, i.e. the money, the job, the body, the girl, the celebrity status. And by society's standards, the definition of success differs for men and women. Traditionally, women have been considered successful if they are thin and beautiful – preferably dangling on the arm of a wealthy man! - while men merely need to be rich and powerful. A fascinating way to measure success, don't you think? But how many of us have actually ever stopped to question this form of brainwashing?

Increasingly, we are led to believe that being successful means being in the public eye. We are bombarded with messaging, both subtle and overt, telling us that unless we have a significant social media profile, then clearly, we are NO-ONE.

It's not enough to simply be great at what you do anymore. You have to shout about it, blog about it, tweet about it, Instagram it, and if you're super lucky, get 'featured 'in the media for it. You've got to be your own self-publicist with 'blogs 'and 'followers', 'likes 'and 'feeds'. And we're not talking small scale here; we are talking BIG, BIG numbers: less than 500,000 and who exactly are you?

You might as well not bother. Right?

Totally wrong.

I want you to know that having all or any of the above doesn't automatically make you successful. Success can be quiet. It can be under the radar, and most importantly, success can be defined on your own terms – as actress and activist Pamela Anderson recently made clear when she announced she was quitting Instagram, Twitter and Facebook. In her final post, she talked of being "free" and hoped that others would "find the strength and inspiration" to follow their own purpose and no longer be seduced by online platforms, because "that's what they want and can use to make money [and] control your brain".

It's time for all of us to challenge our thinking on this because mainstream indicators of success contribute to an imbalanced perception and don't necessarily represent the truth. So, how do we measure success?

You see, I truly believe that success comes from within. You can't buy it, you can't borrow it, and you can't pretend to own it. You can have the biggest house on the street and still have crazy thoughts that make you think you are unsuccessful. You can have the so-called perfect body shape promoted by magazines, diet companies and celebrities, but be sitting on a beach in your bikini feeling utterly miserable. You can have the wife/ husband/ child/ lover but you can still think you are 'less than' anyone else you know.

Success is not about appearance or material possessions; it is entirely an inside job. If you are looking for success, you need to start with your mindset. Often the problem lies with convincing yourself that you are worthy of it.

FAILURE DOESN'T EXIST

Success is such a powerful word. We all want it, we all admire those who appear to have it and we are all terribly scared of the opposite of it. In this day and age, failure is considered a dirty word. We often think in terms of black and white, for example: "if am not successful, I must be a failure."

But this isn't true.

Let's take a look at that word 'failure'. So many people come into my office saying they think they have, in one way or another, failed. It isn't something many people talk about with their friends or spouses over the dinner table, but as a life coach, in the safe and confidential space where I sit with my clients, I hear this a lot from many different people – from CEOs to creatives. But telling yourself you think you are a failure in one way or another, is one of the meanest things you can do to yourself. It creates a feeling of shame, and shame is one of the worst feelings a person can have.

Telling yourself you are a failure for things that are out of your control makes no sense either. The rhetoric in the mind goes like this: The person you like hasn't texted back, so you conclude: "I am a failure." You didn't get the job promotion, therefore, "I am a failure." You couldn't get some tech to work properly: "I am a failure." Your partner wants a divorce: "I am a failure." You get the idea.

My point here is that often what we say to ourselves, we would never ever dream of saying to someone else. If your son or daughter came back from school with a six out of ten on a maths test, you would never say: "That isn't good enough. You are a failure. That result proves you are worthless."

You would never say to your friend who has just told you his wife is leaving him: "No surprise… You are a total failure, mate." So, if you wouldn't say it to someone else, then isn't it about time you stopped saying things like this to yourself?

As a coach, the word 'failure 'simply doesn't exist in my vocabulary. Life is about lessons, growing and learning. It is about evolving and elevating. And no growth can happen without it. If we aren't learning we are stalling, stuck and, very likely, bloody bored. Life would be bland because, simply put, if we aren't out there failing at things, we simply aren't learning and, in turn, cannot ultimately succeed.

Think for a moment how athletes approach failure: they have to lose constantly in order to learn how to win. They have to make mistakes in order to get better. How many times has someone like champion tennis player Novak Djokovic had to fail in order to finally hold that winner's trophy? As of December 2020, he was ranked world No 1, with a record of 17 Grand Slam men's singles titles. He is the undisputed top player of the past decade, yet for almost three years, between 2008 and the end of 2010, he reached only one Grand Slam final, the 2010 U.S. Open.

Instead of defeating him, those failures set him up to ultimately win. He had to fail in order to understand where his weaknesses lay so that he could get better, be better and win.

Dolly Parton is considered one of the world's most successful country music singers and songwriters. Aged 75, she's also an actress, author, businesswoman and humanitarian. As she has said: "I'm not going to limit myself just because people won't accept the fact that I can do something else."

She's also refreshingly candid about her past failures, observing, "I thank God for my failures. Maybe not at the time but after some reflection. I never feel like a failure just because something I tried has failed. The way I see it, if you want the rainbow, you gotta put up with the rain."

In much the same way, success often grows out of adversity. I've never grown from anything that's easy. People used to say to me that we have bad times so that we can appreciate the good. I used to laugh until I started to believe it myself. My hardest times were always the times that propelled me into growing, to self-awareness, to understanding who I was. And looking back, I wouldn't change a thing.

As public figures like fitness superstar Joe Wicks, MBE, and premiership footballer-turned-campaigner Marcus Rashford, MBE, would testify, the hard times test your strength of character and show who you are. Responsible for keeping the nation fit (and sane!) during the first lockdown of 2020 with his daily online workouts, Joe has spoken about how he used sport to relieve stress and escape a difficult home situation growing up on a council estate in Surrey.

"I had a very chaotic upbringing: a lot of shouting and slamming doors – impatience, intolerance, effing and blinding," he said in an interview with You magazine (22/11/2020). "I was a mini version of who I am now, rounding everybody up [his two brothers], telling them, 'Come on, get changed, let's get out there – I can't play football without you! 'That's been a massive part of my life."

Giving back has become a massive part of his life, too, in the same way it has for Manchester United player Marcus, who galvanised the nation with his campaign to supply free school meal vouchers to disadvantaged children during the school holidays. Having relied on free school meals growing up in Manchester, he said he never wanted any other child to have to "feel like I did".

For both men, it's about mindset. The same self-belief that propelled Marcus to the premiership league also spurred him to help others after an injury left him unable to train, coinciding with the start of the coronavirus pandemic in 2020. As he told The Guardian newspaper: "The injury prevented me from doing pretty much anything, so I needed to set my mind on something that would turn a negative into a positive and help those who needed it most."

Similarly, Joe has been open about how exercise helps to improve his mental health and how, when he suffered burnout during the first lockdown, he took up guided meditation to calm his mind. "Before that I was getting into self-pity but I have changed my perspective and it has allowed me to stay more positive," he told the Evening Standard (11/11/2020).

The hard times give you an amazing opportunity to manage your mind. And the key here is mind over matter. We juggle up to 60,000 thoughts a day, so learning to catch the negative ones is very important. We must first start to get conscious of what we are thinking and saying to ourselves. Thoughts pop into our minds all the time and we have a lot more control of the thoughts that we choose than we realise. It's important we try to focus on slowing down our thought processes and work out exactly what we are thinking.

If you are thinking, "I am a total failure", that thought will be creating a lot of negative feelings. Instead, you need to start to question the thought. Ask yourself, "Is this thought about being a failure serving me well or making me feel bad? Is this thought going to get me to the feelings and the results I want?". Of course, it isn't. So, it is time to start questioning how to think about the situation differently, in a more positive way. For example, "If this situation had not happened, I wouldn't have learnt what I am learning now" or "this thing that has happened has taught me about contrast. I have learnt what I don't want in order to know what I do want."

It is also useful to remember our thoughts are not facts. What we think is a fact is often just a thought. Be mindful of what is a fact and what is a thought and be prepared to challenge yourself to think about things differently.

INNER PEACE

You need to get to that place where you can unravel your thought processes, belief systems and indoctrinations to work out what success represents for you.

For me, success means inner peace, achieved through working diligently on my thinking. I was lucky enough to experience life at both the top of the so-called social ladder and the bottom – from having it all in terms of material comforts to barely surviving and living each day for my next 'fix'. Ironically, it was when I was at my lowest and had absolutely nothing to lose that I learnt what was important in life. At that point, staying clean from one day to the next was an accomplishment; I succeeded every time I didn't use drugs. Even if it was just hourly at the start. It was that basic and that profound, and it taught me so much about myself and what I wanted from life.

If you've been willing to grow from a really tough experience, then you can consider yourself successful because you didn't stay stuck in your misery. Look at the circumstances you have had to overcome to get where you are; all the battles and challenges you have faced, and then look back down the mountain at how far you have come. That's a great measure of success.

There are many people out there who are successful because they've never forgotten where they come from and remain grounded as a result. I mentioned Dolly Parton earlier, and she is definitely one of those people. Her story is well documented: how she grew up dirt poor in a one-room shack in

Tennessee that she shared with her parents and 11 siblings, and how, at the age of 18, she took the bus to Nashville to make it as a country star.

Today, she says: "I love the fact that I have a rags-to-riches story. I love that I feel like Cinderella. I take a lot of pride in that…I draw from my childhood. That's what keeps me strong. I'm not ashamed of any part of my life."

She told the Sunday Times Magazine (22/11/2020): "I do feel I have accomplished more than I dreamt of. I dreamt of getting out of the Smoky Mountains. I dreamt of being successful, with my songs. I wanted to be rich, to travel, I wanted to have things I could share. So, I think I'm a very successful person."

She's also wise enough to know that all the wealth in the world won't make you happy, adding: "You can be a star, you can be rich and still be miserable. I enjoy my little self – I never get too far from my little Dolly that I was then. I love watching her grow and be all of those things. But I still feel like I've got bigger dreams to dream."

For Dolly, as for many people who follow their dreams, it's about constantly striving and pushing herself; never giving up or feeling complacent, and always being driven to achieve and do more, yet in a balanced and realistic way.

Another motivating factor is having the resolve to do well without necessarily the talent to ease the way. Former Bank of England governor, Canadian Mark Carney, is an interesting example of someone who showed that early determination to succeed when he played ice hockey at Harvard University. Although he was the men's team's goalie, he was on the subs bench and only ever played one full game. His coach Bill Cleary recalled that it was always the benchwarmers who did well in life. "Over the years, guys like him are the ones who have become successful," he told The Times Magazine (21/11/2020). "The guys with the ability sometimes have too much – they don't know what it is to work."

Many of us will identify with the coach's observation; having to work hard is what motivates and inspires us. In a recent study, business owners were asked what advice they would give to their younger selves – the consensus was: stay motivated, don't give up and be confident. The poll of 1000 small and medium-sized firms also revealed that they could expect to face four years of hard work before finding success.

Strangely, the truth is, if it is too easy to achieve our goals, we miss the point. I believe it is the rocky road, the long and arduous journey, that makes it all worthwhile. Often, it is simply the wanting and working towards the thing you wish to achieve that is actually the most important and joyous part.

How you treat other people is also fundamental to success. And beneficial for both you and them. It feels good to be kind, thoughtful, empathetic and compassionate. When you give back to others and the planet and make a conscious effort to create a positive impact, that's what really counts. Albert Einstein summed it up perfectly when he said: "Try not to become a person of success, but rather try to become a person of value."

Cultivating gratitude is another key indicator of success. Looking at the things we do have instead of the things we don't; being grateful for the journey and for the good things we have experienced along the way, will automatically elevate how we feel. The pandemic has made us more aware than ever of what matters in life and how important it is to be grateful for our health, homes, families, friends and jobs. It has also taught us how to live in the present moment. Being able to appreciate your life now, and not catastrophising or creating disaster scenarios in your head, will help you to realise you can do anything you want. Your only limit is you.

DON'T COMPARE!

One common mistake people make in their pursuit of success is that they often feel compelled to compete against others. If you are building your own business or brand, this is such a waste of time. Believe me, there is enough to go around for everyone. Try to look at competition from a different perspective and see our differences as key to our success – what we are able to offer as individuals is unique but no less or more important than what anyone else can bring to the table, so let's make space for each other. And let's cheer each other on in the process! It feels so much better to let go of a 'scarcity 'mindset (the opposite of an abundance one) and go out into the world with a deep sense of personal worth and security. This is how success happens!

Marcus Rashford has the right attitude. "Only stay in competition with yourself," he told The Guardian (04/01/2021). "Everyone's journey is different. There is no right way to do it. Train hard and believe in yourself."

It really is a drain on our time and energy to constantly compare ourselves with others or worry about what they think of us. As I've said many times before, the truth is you never really know what is going on in other people's lives or behind their closed doors. You just never know. What other people think of you is ultimately something you have no control over, either. Being self-obsessed and worried about what everyone thinks of you isn't the sexiest trait and definitely doesn't help your confidence!

As New York-based psychologist and author Guy Winch wisely says: "Success will never lead to happiness if we lose ourselves in its pursuit. If the cost of success is stress or depression or anxiety or this feeling of never being good enough compared to your classmates, I don't know that that's a healthy definition of success. I don't know that it's the kind of success you should aspire to."

BE A RULE BREAKER

As I've already touched on in this chapter, we are programmed by society to believe that success must look a certain way, and that to achieve it, we must conform at all costs – with nothing in-between. I would argue that the opposite is true and we need to be willing to sometimes break the rules – and go against the norm - in order to create our own definition of success.

Eleanor Roosevelt once said: "Do what you feel in your heart to be right – for you'll be criticised anyway." Finding purpose and doing what we love in life is, perhaps, one of the greatest measures of personal success.

Growing up in an affluent middle-class family, I was taught to believe that to be successful I needed to be thin, wealthy and married with two children. Funnily enough, I don't think I'm not successful now because I didn't buy into that conventional belief system. I've been married and divorced twice (so, been there, done that!), and I don't have children, but I do have a small circle of close friends who make me laugh every single day. And I have a job that I love and have helped thousands of people to change their lives. I guess, I just define my success differently from the tribal thinking.

That doesn't mean my parents were wrong to want those things for me; I simply chose not to fit in for the sake of it. I'm not denying that someone who makes a lot of money is successful but what I'm saying is that this reflects only one aspect of their life. It's like saying you can only be successful if you go around holding an apple in your hand! Which is, of course, absurd, if you think about it.

Material wealth doesn't necessarily equate to self-worth, and achieving that is surely a more important – and enduring - measure. I have clients who run major companies, who tell me they are constantly chasing bigger and bigger deals, but when I ask them if that makes them contented, they'll tell me that they were at their happiest when they were starting out and could enjoy the challenges without all the pressure.

Up until I had been clean for a little while, I didn't have a clue what I was going to do with my life. I had no goals or ambitions and definitely didn't think I was ever going to be successful in a conventional sense. For most of my early working life, I was already regularly using drugs and any job I managed to hold down – mostly secretarial – was simply a means to an end: feeding my habit. I existed in this twilight state from the time I started my first job at 17, all the way through until I had been clean for several years.

As soon as I was drugs-free, though, and had done the work on changing my mindset, it became very clear what I needed to do – it was such a powerful realisation that when I finally 'got it', it was glaringly obvious. I was always meant to become a life coach and help others – it all suddenly made perfect sense! I can hand on heart tell you that it was a 'calling – 'and, happily, I've never looked back. I do believe we are all here for greater things and the Universe has a plan for every one of us. Everything I went through was for a reason: to heal and help.

What my challenging experiences ultimately taught me was how to tap into my inner strength and trust my intuition; I didn't know what I was capable of until I was tested to the extreme. It meant that I was able to move beyond being a 'druggie' or an 'addict'. I didn't want to cling to the label as a strange kind of safety net – I wanted to be free. In fact, this was the reason I finally left recovery because I was determined to live a normal life again. Don't get me wrong, the 12-Step programme saved my life, but I saw many of my fellow addicts choosing to remain there, sitting on the 'bridge', because they were fearful of crossing back into society.

Crossing that metaphorical bridge was one of the hardest things I've ever done in my life. It lost me friendships I'd made while in recovery, but by that point, I believed in myself wholeheartedly and had so many things I wanted to achieve, that I was unstoppable. The ones who chose to end contact did not agree with my decision to leave, while those who remained in touch were non-judgmental – and more able to acknowledge that you could become well enough to leave treatment and follow your own path.

This quote from author and spiritual leader Marianne Williamson's book, A Return To Love, has particular resonance for me: "As we let our own light shine, we unconsciously give other people permission to do the same. As we're liberated from our own fear, our presence automatically liberates others."

Ultimately, success is about finding our passion, our purpose; about doing the things that make us feel free, joyful and peaceful. In order to reach this place, we need to be brave; ready to embrace positive change and willing to put in the hard graft. It's about believing the simple truth that you are enough.

CASE STUDY

An engaging young man walked into my office who had been married about a year with a new baby. He was running his own business but was secretly struggling. He was using drugs and alcohol and kept getting himself into deeper and deeper trouble with his business, his wife etc. He knew if he carried on in this destructive manner he would lose everything. When he arrived at my office, I knew immediately the work we had to do: unravel his unrealistic expectations of himself; teach him the true meaning of success, and help him to learn to value and love himself. We needed to closely examine why he was running towards his addictions and away from himself. We worked together for about six sessions and the change in him by the end was palpable. He was one of those clients who seemed to literally transform from a caterpillar into a butterfly, right in front of my eyes. He was willing to do whatever it took and, believe me, we did some intense work.

He left me this review:

"Jacqueline is amazing and made a massive difference to my life in a short space of time!

She believed in me and helped me to find the power to love myself and overcome the bad behaviours which were holding me back. I'm a different person now with great belief in myself and I take everything that life throws at me in my stride. The help she has given me is priceless and I can't thank her enough."

WORKSHEET

Social conditioning plays a large part in how we see ourselves and our place in the world. It also gives us an extremely narrow definition of the word 'success', which can have a major impact on our confidence and wellbeing. Ask yourself the following questions to redefine what success means to you. - you might be surprised:

What did your upbringing teach you that you had to do or be in order to be a 'success'?

_____

_____

_____

Which of those things have you achieved?

_____

_____

_____

Which of those things haven't you managed to achieve?

_____

_____

_____

Do you believe you are not successful because you have not mastered those things?

_____

_____

_____

Who taught you to think this way? And who taught them?!

_____

_____

_____

Now list ten things you have done that you think could also be viewed as a success?

_____

_____

_____

When you look at that list and read it back, I want you to imagine that it has been written by someone else – would you then think that they were successful?

_____

_____

_____

Now work out three different thoughts about success that instinctively feel more suited to who you are as a person

_____

_____

_____

How do you feel now about success?

_____

_____

_____

CHAPTER ELEVEN

HOW TO TRULY BELIEVE IN YOURSELF

Do you want to believe in yourself and in your ability to achieve whatever you want?

After decades of working in personal development, one thing I know for sure is that before anyone starts on their own journey of self-discovery, they will be holding a limiting belief along the lines of… "I am not good enough". It is something so many people are guilty of thinking and which they live with day in, day out. We berate ourselves over the smallest of things, constantly feeling as though we haven't reached our full potential and are, in turn, responsible for holding ourselves back in some way. We know something is not quite right but we just can't seem to break this punishing cycle.

What I want to say here is that every client I have ever seen has been mistaken in their thoughts about this. Because we *are* all born good enough, and with the right guidance, we CAN change our negative thought patterns and achieve great things.

We all hold mixed opinions of ourselves and it's quite normal to experience emotions like fear and anxiety when faced with challenges. It's how you harness these feelings that counts. When you believe in yourself, you are able to turn fear into action because you have a goal or vision for your life that you truly believe is achievable. However, if you suffer from low self-esteem, you are less likely to act, which can be both debilitating and restricting.

Self-esteem is such an integral part of who we are. It's the overall belief we have and hold about ourselves and the value we place on ourselves as people. If you consciously or even subconsciously believe you are not good enough and your overall opinion is that you are inadequate or inferior and therefore, "undeserving", then life can become one big struggle. A lack of self-belief or self-confidence will impact your relationships, your career and your personal development and keep you feeling trapped and small. It absolutely doesn't need to be like that, though.

SELF-LOVE

In my humble opinion, learning self-love is the foundation for all the other things you want in life. It is the key to believing in yourself and unlocking your uniqueness.

We have to learn to love ourselves first and foremost before we can reach our true potential and really flourish. Simply put, self-love is the answer to just about everything.

It's ironic, really, how we set about looking for love from our partners, our parents and our friends; we seem to look for it everywhere except, of course, from ourselves. Why do we find this so difficult?

Well, we are all the product of our conditioning and training, so we need to identify where and how we learnt to think we weren't good enough or deserving enough in the first place. Our opinions are ingrained in us by the society and culture we grow up in, and can sometimes limit our potential if we allow them.

For example, if you are told from a young age to accept your lot in life and that you have no control over your destiny, you might believe that there is little point in trying to create a different life. If you are repeatedly warned you will go to Hell if you do something wrong or make a mistake, then you are most likely going to grow up full of fear and insecurity.

Girls, in particular, are subject to brainwashing: the idea of becoming a mother is passed down through centuries of social conditioning, so that if a woman chooses not to have children, she is viewed as abnormal or "less than". In the same way, girls are taught by their mothers (who, in turn, were instructed by their mothers) to believe that in order to be considered worthy by society, they need to conform to a particular body shape – invariably, a slender one! This message is further reinforced by social media, which exploits the insecurities of young girls and women by showcasing unrealistic "perfect lives".

As I always say, perfection does not exist. But what you have to remember is that everyone is trying to sell you something. And one of the main ways that companies push their products is to make sure that you don't feel "good enough" about yourself so someone can sell you a solution to that perceived problem.

We are led to believe that our wellbeing is dependent on external factors, such as achieving a certain weight; owning a bigger house or a new car; nailing that high-powered job, making a shed-load of money or finding the perfect partner.

The advertising industry (which increasingly targets us through social media platforms) is geared around the premise that, if you buy this or that product, then you will "feel better/happier/thinner/smarter", etc, and therefore, be considered successful – in modern society's eyes.

We've all experienced the dopamine kick of instant gratification that buying some desired piece of jewellery or clothing produces, but it's only ever a temporary sensation and no substitute for the sense of inner happiness that comes from self-acceptance and self-love.

If you believe you can access happiness from outside of yourself, you are in for disappointment. Trying to cultivate self-worth from anywhere other than within yourself makes zero sense and will not work.

When clients come to me and say they don't feel "good enough", my question to them is always, "Why wouldn't you believe in yourself?" We're not born *not* to be our own cheerleader in life, but for some reason, we seem to think it is okay for others to decide our self-worth, and at some stage during childhood, we hand over our power in the hope that we will be validated. We let society dictate how we feel about ourselves and often use it as an excuse not to take responsibility for our lives. This is particularly the case if you are British; we Brits hesitate to put our head above the parapet for fear of what other people might think of us. Stiff upper lip and all that. We are too busy trying to fit in, rather than trusting our intuition.

America's first female vice-president, Kamala Harris, is someone who has always refused to fit in for the sake of adhering to societal norms. She was taught by her single parent mother, a scientist and civil rights activist, that ambition was something to celebrate because it showed a sense of purpose and determination. As we all know, Kamala's resolute belief in herself has more than paid off: she has achieved a series of exceptional 'firsts' in her life – from becoming the first black female attorney-general of California to only the second African American woman and the first South Asian American to serve in the United States Senate.

Yet, if she'd listened to the naysayers, she would not now be the highest-ranking female official in U.S. history. In her journey to the White House, she was constantly told she was "too much"; too ambitious, especially for a woman, according to her equally driven niece, author and activist Meena Harris. "People said [to Kamala]: 'You're too young. You're too much of a woman. Frankly, you're too black.' She never listened to any of it," Meena revealed in an interview with The Times Magazine (23/01/2021). "And now we're able to show everybody that it's possible. We've broken that glass ceiling. Ambition succeeded. We won."

Meena also made this insightful observation: "We're conditioned to internalise these things, and we need a reminder of unlearning, relearning and reclaiming power, space, voice and ambition, too."

As I've set out to explain in this book, managing our own minds is how we take back control and restore power to ourselves. We may not all have had Kamala's role model mother, but we can *learn* to unlearn and relearn. Always remember, a thought is not a fact, so if you hold negative or limiting thoughts about yourself, look for evidence that the opposite is true. It will become more difficult to believe a thought when you have the evidence to prove the opposite is actually true!

We all know people who seem innately confident. It's one of those things that we think others are 'lucky' to have; like they have this special superpower that those consumed by self-doubt can only dream about. They seem to have it all: they can hold their own in a room, are admired by others, and their positivity and energy seem to promote and inspire confidence in everyone they meet. They come across as people who are at peace with themselves, who face their fears head-on and couldn't care less what anyone else thinks about them. They are also more likely to fulfill their potential because they will go after what they want, whether a promotion or new job, because they know they are more than capable of succeeding. In contrast, someone else might pass up a job opportunity because they have already decided they are not good enough.

KNOW YOUR WORTH

So how does that work? How are some people so confident and what is it they have that others think they don't?

Simply put, they *really, truly* believe in themselves.

If you have this elusive quality, you will know your true worth and value. You will be the agent of your own success, and by that, I don't mean your life will be an uninterrupted straight line of enviable win after win. But you will be able to access reserves of inner strength when most needed and you will see challenges as a chance to learn new skills and gain a greater understanding of yourself.

Critical to building this self-belief is becoming your own number one fan or best friend. The point here is that when you love others, you treat them well. So why not start to treat yourself like you would your best friend?

I'm not saying you need to be fully in love with yourself overnight; that's neither practical nor realistic. But it's essential to stop beating yourself up or judging yourself before you can move towards a place of acceptance. After you have accepted who you are - your unique and authentic self - you can begin to build your confidence and start to become your own champion.

Let me be clear what I mean about the word 'love' here. I don't mean the ego type of love as in "I am amazing and everyone else is below me"; that is not what I am talking about. There is a difference between liking yourself and being a narcissist! What I mean is soul level love - like the love you would show for a child, where you see the good; where you practice patience and kindness, and where you are rooting for them to be the best they can be. That's the type of love I want you to have for yourself: empowering, positive and uplifting.

It is about being conscious and aware, accepting you're not perfect (remember, good enough is really good enough, despite what social media would have you believe to the contrary!), and being grateful for what you do have in life – your health, your family, your home, your job etc.

We've all got the potential to do great things (I truly believe the Universe has bigger plans for us than we sometimes realise) but, frankly, unless we consciously tap into that potential and are prepared to do the work that it takes, through intense self-development and mindful spiritual practises, then nothing is going to change – and our relationships, our home lives and our careers will continue to suffer.

Many people worry that when they start to "go there" in therapy or coaching they will open a Pandora's Box of emotional troubles. The truth is, it is never as hard as you think. You just have to be willing to examine your inner self if you really want to change. And change is possible. Why resign yourself to living a half-life agonising about what everyone else thinks about you, when you know that you could live completely differently: confident, free and fulfilled?

In order to understand yourself better, you need to be open to making mistakes along the way and try to learn from them. This is how we become stronger and more resilient – and GROW.

Everybody goes through rough times, whether a bad break-up, losing a job or saying goodbye to a beloved pet; they are just a part of life. At times, it can feel like we're being hammered by one blow after another, but these are all life lessons and what is important is that you don't let the negative experiences define who you are.

In fact, I would go so far as to say that they are actually some of the best 'classroom' moments you can have because they give you a choice to either remain stuck in that unhappy space, where you feel everything and everyone is against you, or you can take on board the lessons they deliver, strengthen your mindset and move forward.

LEARN FROM YOUR MISTAKES

Don't get me wrong. I understand from my own traumatic experiences how our minds can tend to go to negative places and get wrapped up in the moment, but this will only attract other negative influences into your life. It comes back to the old saying, "What goes around comes around". If you put negative energy out into the universe, you're going to get negative energy back. It's like plugging a hole you feel inside you in all the wrong places.

There's that famous quote by American pioneer and industrialist Henry Ford, who said: "Whether you think you can, or you think you can't – you're right". The point he was making was how much a person's attitude can determine success or failure. Scientific studies have shown that if you judge yourself to be capable of success, this will increase your chances of actual success. You're also more likely to be able to learn from your mistakes and bounce back from failure. Whereas, if you have little belief in your ability to complete a task successfully, you will most probably fail before you even start towards a goal - you simply won't be able to imagine a positive outcome.

J.K. Rowling, author of the juggernaut Harry Potter franchise, is the perfect example of someone who overcame difficult life experiences by swapping limiting beliefs for empowering ones. With a reported fortune of more than £795 million, according to The Sunday Times Rich List (2020), and record-breaking book sales, she is undisputedly one of the world's most successful authors. But despite her phenomenal success, she considered herself a failure in her mid-twenties: her marriage had collapsed and she was a single mother living on welfare in a tiny apartment in Edinburgh. Things got so bad at one stage, she even contemplated suicide.

She could have stayed in a place of feeling bad about herself, dwelling on what went wrong with her marriage and what she could have done differently. Instead, she decided to see her failures as liberating, giving her the chance to focus on her passion: writing – she famously wrote much of her first book, Harry Potter and the Philosopher's Stone, in a café while her baby daughter was napping in her pram. Even then, she faced rejection, with her work being knocked back 12 times before she managed to get a publishing deal. The rest is history.

The outspoken author has always been candid about how she turned her life around and embraced failure rather than running away from it. "Failure taught me things about myself that I could have learned no other way," she has said. "I discovered that I had a strong will, and more discipline than I had suspected. It is impossible to live without failing at something, unless you live so cautiously that you might as well not have lived at all – in which case, you fail by default."

For Rowling, it all came down to mindset: "Anything is possible if you have enough nerve. You control your own life. Your own will is extremely powerful."

When I look back at almost every negative experience I've had in my life, it has always opened up a door to something new and better. That's not to say I haven't had moments of self-pity when I would throw my toys out of the pram and think, how much more of this drama do I need to endure? My grandmother used to say, "This too shall pass", whether good times or bad, and it's something I've never forgotten.

Surviving hardship or trauma is how we become who we are meant to be. It is the route we have to take to reach a place of real inner peace and happiness. We cannot get there without it!

Setbacks are a part of the journey. For every one you experience, there will be something else that pushes you forward. I remember standing in London's Baker Street when I started my life coaching clinic, handing out flyers at 5.30am outside a well-known gym. I got more dates than clients - which was both frustrating and, of course, funny - but I was willing to persevere because I believed in myself and knew that I would eventually succeed. I hadn't come this far and overcome so many challenges, not to succeed. There was no social media back then, so I had to rely on personal networking and word-of-mouth, but I was confident that whoever was meant to come knocking at my door would do so – and more than 7000 clients later, I know that it was because I had faith in myself that I have got to where I am today. I'm absolutely convinced that what drew people to me was the fact that I *believed* in myself; they could see that I had been through my own wild journey and there was no faking it.

As you can probably tell by now, I am big on both talking the talk *and* walking the walk!

BE KIND TO YOURSELF

I can't stress enough, though, how important it is to be kind to yourself along the way – and patient! When I was in recovery for drug addiction, I could only take it one tiny step at a time. I would look at the clock from the moment I got up and would tell myself, "I won't take drugs now at 7am, but if I want them at 8am, then I will." Then 8am would come and I would say, "I have done one whole hour, I can surely make it to 9am." And so on. Hour-by-hour, I was gradually able to tick off drug-free days, weeks and months. Unsurprisingly, I spent a lot of time during that first difficult year clock-watching!

The same applies if you are in recovery for any other sort of struggle or addiction. If you are an alcoholic and stop drinking for one day, focus on the fact that you were able to give it up for one whole day. That is a massive achievement! You can do anything one day at a time. This will help to build your confidence and give you the incentive to keep going. The point is to never give up trying because you *are* worth it; good enough is really good enough.

You see, life has a funny way of delivering just what you need at the right time – as long as you have done your work and are open and receptive to receiving whatever comes your way. It is how you *respond* in any given situation that is key. If you are cognitively flexible – able to change what you are thinking about and how you are thinking about it – you will be able to better handle new and unexpected circumstances, and therefore, more likely to thrive. As the great naturalist Charles Darwin once said: "It's not the strongest of the species that survives, nor the most intelligent, it is the one most adaptable to change."

Instead of applying a thought process along the lines of, "What if this doesn't work out?", rephrase the question to ask yourself, "What if it does?". You could even say, "If this doesn't work out, what is the worst thing that will happen?". Control what you are able to control – not what is outside of your power. This is something business leaders are often quick to grasp. When the boss of easyJet, Johan Lundgren, was asked how he planned to bounce back from the pandemic following company losses of more than £800 million along with 4500 jobs, he replied: "It helps to remember that while you can't control what happens to you, you can always control your response." He also compared his battle to Ernest Hemingway's The Old Man and the Sea: "It is about a man who faces challenge after challenge but he keeps his mood and rises up again," he told the Evening Standard (26/01/2021).

When you are ready to tap into your inner resilience, you will find you are much more capable of dealing with adversity than you realised. Embracing a flexible mindset is what matters. But, remember, resilience is like a muscle that needs to be developed. It is in the act of managing whatever the problem or obstacle is that *builds* your resilience

I can honestly say that I have become stronger, braver and wiser with each passing year - nowhere more evident than in my attitude towards romantic relationships. For years, I kept dating unsuitable men. No matter how toxic the relationship, I never seemed to learn. I kept going back for more. The truth is, I didn't know any better. I only knew unhealthy love because I didn't feel good enough; I didn't feel I deserved to be treated with respect and kindness. So, how did I escape that self-destructive cycle?

I had to endure breakdowns to achieve break-throughs. I had to get to a place that hurt so much, where I was sick and tired of repeating the same patterns of self-destructive behaviour, in order to change my feelings about love. I had to start looking at love in all its complexities and learn to let go of the negative thoughts I held about it and, subsequently, about myself. I had to learn to understand a new kind of love that was very different to anything I had ever experienced before. I had to accept that love was not frightening or terrifying and that I wouldn't lose myself if I opened myself up to it.

Of course, it began with my mindset, and the more I learnt to unlearn what I had been taught and re-learn what was healthy and positive, the more my life started to improve. Remember, if you don't love yourself, then how can you expect anyone else to love you? You have to be willing to do the work. It took time and hard slog; it took being brave and honest and determined. I had to create personal boundaries – emotional and physical - and ask others to respect them. I found this Instagram quote to be particularly apt: "The only people who are likely to suggest that setting a boundary is selfish are the people who are benefiting from you having none." I had to learn from scratch what a healthy relationship was and it was one of the biggest lessons in my life.

Gradually, I started to attract completely different types of men. I went from abusive, unavailable, confusing, exhausting, and ultimately, toxic relationships to ones with men, who were truly kind, deeply considerate, loving, conscious and connected – not to mention *available*. The thing is I could never have dated these men if I hadn't put in all the work on myself. The man I am dating today is a diamond. He is totally different to my previous 'type', and the truth is, I would probably never have gone for him in the past. It was only when I did my inner work, that I realised my previous 'type' was precisely what was getting me into trouble. Learning to change my thoughts, patterns and behaviours around love was the key that unlocked my roadblock to real love, and these days, behaviour I once considered to be acceptable, most definitely, no longer is.

I can honestly say I am 100 percent happier and more fulfilled as a result.

INVEST IN YOURSELF

There are many practical ways in which you can invest in your most important asset, YOU.

Firstly, I would strongly recommend seeing a coach so you can be guided in your journey to self-love. A good coach will help you work on your thoughts – what you need to unlearn and re-learn and how to change your mindset. It is so important to properly examine the detail of your own situation and look at why you perpetuate negative thoughts about yourself.

Secondly, I would suggest surrounding yourself with people who inspire and support you, and love you for who you are. This is a vital form of self-care. Constantly being around people who don't really have your back and are merely friends out of convenience, is not going to do much for your sense of self-esteem. Deep and lasting friendship is what matters.

Also remember to embrace moments of joy, however small or fleeting. Sounds obvious but sometimes we forget. Even when things seem tough, there will be moments – whether it's a loving conversation with a friend or a stranger being kind to you – that will help to lift your spirits. It's important to acknowledge when this happens and say to yourself: "Not everything is bad, and I can and I will come out on the other side." Every day you're alive is a blessing and being able to express gratitude is life-affirming.

Thirdly, be firm about creating personal boundaries so that you can make time to switch off, whether it's putting your mobile phone out of reach at night or saying 'no'. This doesn't make you unlikable or mean; it makes you smart. If you really want to love yourself, you will not 'people please'. Loving yourself means showing self-respect and prioritising what *you* want to do. It's your choice. Try saying 'no' just once a day and see how you feel!

Lastly, keep learning and striving. This is fundamental to believing in yourself. Learning nourishes my soul and makes me happy. In the words of the great Ancient Greek philosopher Aristotle, "The more you learn, the more you realise how much you don't know."

CASE STUDY

A young woman once came to see me, who appeared to have it all – at least, on the surface. She had a great job, a supportive group of friends and enough disposable income to buy pretty much whatever she wanted, but she felt miserable. She just didn't believe in herself and that lack of belief was preventing her from living a full and happy life. She would go to work, go home, and hardly ever socialised. When she did, she felt anxious and nervous. We did a lot of work together on unravelling her thoughts and what emerged was that deep-down, she didn't think she was good enough. When we looked into this, it became evident she had learnt to think this way as a child. She had consistently been told by her parents that whatever grade she achieved at school, she should have "done better". When we managed to identify the source of this negative thinking pattern and found the evidence to disprove her misplaced belief about not being good enough, she became a different person. She sent me this email: "Jacqueline, just wanted to let you know my life has got BIG!! I am really starting to feel so confident that the guy I have liked for ages finally asked me out. I said 'yes' and we have been dating now for a while. He asked me to meet his friends last night and I went along feeling calm and collected - and without any anxiety! I now love myself, accept myself and fully understand that I cannot control anyone else's thinking, and that's okay by me. They can all think what they want! It is literally liberating. THANK YOU!!!"

WORKSHEET:

Make a list of 12 things you like, appreciate, respect and even love about you. This is about changing your thinking patterns and starting to see yourself in the same way that the people who love you do. Put down everything you can think of to make sure you fill up the list.

_____

_____

_____

_____

_____

_____

_____

_____

_____

_____

Now write a list of all the positive and wonderful things your best friend would say about you if they were talking about your personality, character and why she/he loves you (if you don't know, ask them to send you their list!).

My best friend would say... E.g. I have a great sense of humour

_____

_____

_____

_____

_____

_____

_____

_____

Work on one thought a day that helps you to find some form of self-acceptance and self-belief. For example, "Today, I am going to say to myself, 'I am doing well for my age!'"

ACKNOWLEDGEMENTS

I want to thank my mom, dad and sister. Without them being them I wouldn't be me.

The Redbarts and The Simons - family is everything. Thank you to all of you individually for your continued love and support.

NA, AA, CA, Sue my first therapist, Ashley my second, Martin briefly but all 3 in one way or another spoke words that ultimately saved my life.

Earl for asking me my name, I hope always to remain your princess.

Chris for your support and love from 'the off'. Ray for your time, energy and love.

Ninja Bear for everything. You are my rock and my sister. Alice, Claudine and Zoe because the 4 of you are my foundations.

Pieter because our daily belly laughter and love of all the best things in life keep me sane.

Alexis because we keep it real. Jonathan because you believed in me from the start.

Suzanne because we have shared so much and continue to do so with real love and understanding.

David M because you taught me so much about love.

Juliet Herd for being the loveliest editor making this project effortless.

Corey for your chill LA energy and your 'nothing is a problem 'attitude in getting this book published!

Then, to all the people who tried to bring me down, hurt me, break me, embarrass me, abandon me, abuse me, ridicule me, shame me or belittle me you guys definitely need a thank you, because each of you were the ingredients for the making of me, my strength and all my success.

And lastly the Covid Pandemic for giving me the time to actually write this book.

CLIENT PRAISE FOR THE AUTHOR

"There are times in your life when you need a voice of reason and someone to help you decipher 'the noise' of what is important and what is not...for me, it's gold shoes! Jacqueline has been that person on several occasions and I can say that if it wasn't for her tough love and gentle guidance I would not be walking tall with a smile on my face right now. Thank you, thank you."

"I have had 6 sessions with Jacqueline and I can honestly say it's been life changing. She has a great insight into what's really going on and has assisted in changing my life for the better. I would 100% recommend her to anyone wanting to improve themselves."

"Unquestionably the most effective coach out there today. Whatever your goals your aims your desires your needs anxieties Jacqueline is such an incredible listener and understands how to target the root of the issue and create outcomes that usually would take years to achieve from alternative modalities therapy or treatments. Couldn't recommend her highly enough."

"Jacqueline is a wonderful and very talented coach. She identified the heart of the issues I was struggling with and immediately got to work on breaking them down, allowing me to see the reality of what I was facing, why it was happening and – most importantly – what I could do to change it. I found her approach deeply honest, applicable, practical and extremely effective. You have to do your homework, but it's worth it! Her guidance and support not only allowed me to resolve the initial 'problem' I contacted her to deal with, but also gave me the skills and tools to tackle other issues and generally improve my thought processes and mindset. I'm delighted to now be so empowered and would not hesitate to recommend Jacqueline to anyone who is ready to tackle a change – it can be done!"

"Jacqueline is an amazing person and a brilliant coach. Her no-nonsense, straight talking but ultimately sensitive and empathetic approach is exactly what I needed to work through the particular issue I came to her with. I couldn't recommend working with Jac highly enough!"

"Jacqueline is amazing at what she does; she is thoroughly professional and the best in her field. I highly recommend her and if you are trying to stop smoking she is definitely the one you should go to."

"Jacqueline - I just wanted to say how much I have appreciated our time together over the last few weeks. You really are a very special force of nature. No doubt you've been told this many times before because it is a self- evident truth. Still I want to add to the chorus as I was a lucky beneficiary. Our conversations cleared a lot of stuff away and made room for lots more that came tumbling out. It feels like this is still in progress and it's really very exciting. Whatever next?

"Thanks so much to you Jacqueline for completely shaping my outlook on life and helping me massively along the way!!! I owe everything to you and will definitely be recommending you to everybody I know. Seeing Jacqueline regularly has been the best investment I've ever made, she's so real and honest and caring and it's so nice to have that when seeing someone. Thank you again!!!"

"We all have an inner being to guide us through life. Sometimes, however, life's twists and turns can misdirect that inner being. Jacqueline can help anyone to rediscover their path to joy and their ability to achieve personally and professionally fulfilling lives."

"I researched lots of life coaches and decided to go and see Jacqueline as when I read her website I felt like she would be someone who could help me. When I had my first session with her I walked out with an immediate calm and peace that I had never felt before. She challenged my thinking and my beliefs and after three sessions I felt like the clouds had lifted and life was exciting again. I would recommend her to anyone struggling she really is an amazing life coach!"

"Before seeing Jacqueline, I felt that loving myself would be an endless uphill battle with no hope in sight. After seeing her for the first few sessions, I felt the clouds parting in my head and a new perspective on life being shed. She is the reason I can now live the rest of my life in love and respect of myself. She's given me a new way of looking at the world and the mirror - and at such a young age, I am eternally grateful!"

"Jacqueline has taught me to see life from a different perspective and given me back my self-confidence at a time when I was feeling low and doubted myself in my job. What she teaches you can be applied to everyday life and I cannot thank her enough for this. In under 8 sessions, she has changed how I see other, the world around me and myself!"

"I have been going to Jacqueline for several months now and even after my first session, my outlook on everything totally changed. I feel like a new person who can take on anything and I could not have done it without her. So, thank you Jacqueline for everything - you are the best."

"I have to say that working with Jacqueline has been one of the best decisions I have made. I was going through a really tough time mentally and Jacqueline really helped me see some perspective and how I should view myself and others around me in a much more coherent way. I'd certainly recommend."

"Jacqueline is one of the most extraordinary people I have met. Every single person could benefit from some time with her."

"Jacqueline has been really good for me. I now look at things in a different way and my life has improved in so many areas. She is honest and humorous but above all very genuine. I thoroughly recommend."

"In the beginning I was sceptical about how much Life Coaching could help me and whether it was worth my time/money. However, since I started 6 months ago today, I honestly feel like I have transformed into a completely different person. My whole perspective on life has actually changed and I am now so much more in control of my life. Jacqueline made me realise so many things about my own life which I had not even thought about or considered which were affecting me. Whilst it does take a few sessions to get there, this new way of thinking is something that will definitely benefit me for life! Jacqueline has helped me bring so much more happiness into my life... and for that, however many years down the line, I will always be eternally grateful!"

"Jacqueline is honestly incredible. Her approach challenged me to see things differently whilst allowing me to work at my own pace. The outcome was some massive changes for the better. I'm very grateful."

"I feel extremely lucky and privileged to have met Jacqueline now and not a minute later! Spending time with her working through my shortcomings is the best investment I ever made. Jacqueline has helped me so much after just a few sessions. I am dealing with situations – that would have otherwise been unmanageable for me and would have destroyed me emotionally – in a way that I never thought I was capable of. I am able to calmly and firmly stand up for myself and I am coming out of tough moments stronger, more confident and more empowered than ever. I will be forever grateful to Jacqueline for guiding me in this beautiful journey of learning how to redirect my thoughts and take control of my emotions which is enabling me to turn my perception of situations around for the better and in turn really improving my life. By the way, the sessions are SO much fun; it is very uplifting to be around Jacqueline. I cannot wait to continue to work with her and see more results. I highly recommend her, so don't doubt: go see her, spend the time, do the work. You will only regret not having done it earlier!"

"Jacqueline is the positive female voice I missed out on growing up. Her strength and confidence are infectious. Her ability to help and guide me through my myriad of 'beat myself up' thoughts by turning them into 'I got this life thing' thoughts has been freeing. I still have the odd negative moments, but I'm not scared anymore and can easily work my way through to a point where I'm not overwhelmed with doubt."

"I booked some sessions in with Jacqueline again this year, this time to deal with my total fear of public speaking. I wanted to public speak but when I would get to the event I would be overcome with erratic shallow breathing, trembling, unable to gather my thoughts and awful nausea. So, I turned down every opportunity because the physical reaction to the fear was so strong. After our hypnotherapy sessions I did a kids' assembly and really enjoyed it, no issues with breathing, trembling etc. Then 6 months after that I have just done a talk to 70 people. As it had been a while I wondered how it would go. I had zero nerves and thoroughly enjoyed the whole experience, I loved it and can't wait to do more. Thank you, Jacqueline!"

"This lady is incredible, in just one session so much of my perspective on life changed. As someone who also works closely with her in the industry, I could not recommend her services more. She has worked the last 20 years to now find herself cemented as one of the industry's elite and most well renowned coaches. No matter what you are facing, this woman will help you heal and grow and see from a completely different mindset. Well worth the investment."

"I smoked for 23 years and TODAY is one year since I had my session to stop smoking and I am now ONE YEAR smoke free!!! Thank you so much Jacqueline, what a difference you made!!!"

"I loved working with Jacqueline. I've had a couple of sessions with Jacqueline, her expertise helped point out a lot of suppressed emotions that were blocking me from moving forward in my life. Jaqueline's warmth, love and care made me feel safe to open up and inspired me to have more compassion towards myself and others. Love and appreciate her sessions so much. Working with Jaqueline gave me the confidence I needed to take the first steps in starting my own brand!"

"Jacqueline worked her magic and helped me sort through my thoughts about numerous things. We had never met before and I found it easier to speak with a complete stranger and not hold back. We rearranged how I should/could/would think about things and it's made a huge difference in my day to day life. I highly recommend you try her out and you will see for yourself."

"I don't think words can ever be used to describe my gratitude and admiration for Jacqueline. I cannot fully express the kindness and compassion she's shown me whilst being so instrumental in helping me change my life. She's honest and she just gets it. I'm so excited for my future now knowing that I am in control of the way I feel, and that her door is always open. I cannot speak more highly of her sessions, I am thankful for that first phone call and inspired to achieve half of the success that she has!"

"One of the best life decisions I have ever made. Jacqueline is honest, fair and hard-working. Her humour and "realness" made me look forward to every meeting. She doesn't skip a step, dismiss anything or leave any stone unturned, there are no short-cuts or quick fixes. Her knowledge of the space she's working within and her experience speaks volumes. She has empowered me to be a more honest, kind and compassionate human - not only for others but most importantly, to myself as well. 'Thank you' will never quite be enough and I feel so grateful to have been able to work with her."

"Jacqueline is a fantastic coach, she is able to quickly create a safe environment for you to delve deep and work through the matters which are holding you back or no longer serving you well. I highly recommend Jacqueline."

"Jacqueline Hurst is really impressive and I would recommend her to anyone, in fact I already have. After half an hour with Jacqueline I was able to see the areas of my life that was impacting me, bringing down and affecting my future. Her techniques are great, very realistic and achievable. She's helped me understand and release my potential."

"Professional, supportive and insightful, Jacqueline is fantastic to work with. She gets to the heart of the matter and empowers you to take control. I always leave feeling brighter, more positive and armed with practical steps I can make at home. I'd recommend Jacqueline to anyone who is struggling or just wants some additional support. I'm so grateful for her support!"

"Thanks to Jacqueline I have gained a new, improved perspective for which I will always grateful. She taught me how to see through the hurdles, focus less on insecurity and understand how much can be gained from an open mindset. All of the steps forward in my work and home life can easily linked back to the tools and support that Jacqueline has given me since we started working together. If you have come as far as to be reading this, seriously, just pick up the phone and book a session."

"Jacqueline is an exceptional life coach and has completely changed the way I see myself. I went to her feeling like I was a failure in lots of respects and somehow Jacqueline got me to focus on all the wonderful things I can do and who I really am. Her approach is direct, honest and highly supportive and I really needed someone to give me a reality check to remind me of what is important in life. She is so good at what she does and reaches you when other therapists or coaches have failed. I have recommended Jacqueline to colleagues who are equally complimentary about her skills. If you want someone to get to the issue quickly who can give you techniques that are long lasting and life changing Jacqueline is your woman! Thank you, Jacqueline, you are inspirational."

"Jac gave me the tools to change my life. Everyone could do with her in their life. I cannot recommend her enough. She positively challenges you to change, grow and develop yourself. She brings a new perspective to how you think. I remember clearly the day I walked into her office and I honestly don't think I'd be where I am today without her. I am very grateful for her and all the guidance she has provided me to date."

"Jacqueline will ask you all the right questions to get to the heart of the matter you really need help with - all in a non-judgemental, supportive and nurturing way. She is there for her clients to succeed!!"

"I cannot THANK this woman enough for being truly inspirational, helpful, loving, caring and overall for turning my life around!!!! Jacqueline is up there with some of the most amazing people I have ever met and I really think if you have the opportunity to meet and work with her then you SHOULD! She's so honest and easy going and adapts to any kind of person or problem and I'm so thankful to have her in my life. Funnily enough she has actually become one of my great, great friends. Her sessions are never clinical or routine or fake and that's what I love most about her! Thank you thank you thank you and I'm so happy to have met you."

"Working with Jacqueline has been a life changer for me. She totally 'got me' and helped me change my thought pattern quickly. I used to feel anxious and nervous a lot of the time and since working with her I feel totally free, confident and super happy. Best life coach in London!"

"Jacqueline I am so grateful to have come across such an inspiring soul. You have not only helped me to see the best version of myself but also help me prioritise what is most important to me. Investing in Life Coaching was the best decision I have made. Thank you for your time because honestly, I would never look back again!"

"Jacqueline Hurst is an incredible Life Coach and her work is truly life changing. The best part is how quickly you see results as Jacqueline has an innate ability to thoroughly access and understand your situation with clarity and therefore you get straight to work and no time is wasted. Jacqueline is highly skilled and her techniques work; she is also super friendly, incredibly encouraging and extremely passionate about helping people change their lives for the better. I highly recommend Jacqueline and feel so grateful to have found her!"

"Jacqueline will change your life! I cannot recommend her highly enough. She has given me the tools to lead a life I never imagined possible; she's the best investment you could ever make."

"Literally can't say enough about Jacqueline. She gets it, she's unbelievably wise and insightful. Having a chat with

Jacqueline is inspiring and gives incredible clarity. Anyone and everyone would benefit from speaking with her!"

"Jacqueline is incredible, she has honestly changed my life. Her approach is fantastic, I've been to see numerous therapists without success but I'll never go to another therapist again. Thank you, Jacqueline!"

"Jacqueline is an incredible life coach. She has literally changed my life. Her office is relaxed and open and her coaching technique and style got me sorted out in a matter of weeks. I recommend her highly to anyone who needs even the smallest amount of help. She is truly amazing."

"I can't recommend Jacqueline highly enough. She's brilliant and an amazing life coach! She has positively changed my outlook on life. Her ability to be so astute at picking up a problem has had a profound positive impact on how I live. She will get you 'unstuck'. Her knowledge regarding the human psyche is extensive and I would recommend anyone to go and see her about anything you're struggling with. I'm exceedingly grateful that I came across her serendipitously."

"Jacqueline has a way of empowering others with confidence, happiness, and control. Within a few sessions with Jac, I felt like I had more control over my life. My decisions become easier, my stress became less and my relationships improved. Highly recommend this boss woman to anyone looking to improve their world! Thank you."

"My clients who have seen Jacqueline have experienced extraordinary transformations which Jacqueline has helped them achieve. She is an exceptional coach and can really help people to exceed their expectations of what is possible and be the best version of themselves."

"Jacqueline helped me to transform some very negative and unhelpful thoughts and attitudes I had about myself and my life within a short amount of time. After our sessions, I felt so much more positive, centred and confident and I had a better perspective and direction about various debilitating matters. This was a careful investment that I decided to make on myself and Jacqueline came through. She was exactly what I needed after I made a conscious decision that I wanted and needed change. I am very pleased to of met and worked with such a remarkable lady. She is definitely the real deal and I would highly recommend her."

"Jacqueline is totally and utterly magic! It's hard to put my experience into the correct words but what I do know is that she has changed my life. My experiences have been incredibly powerful and for the first time in years, I believe in in myself and the way my life is falling into place. I feel overwhelmingly grateful to have found her and I could not recommend Jacqueline' services more."

"It is difficult to put into words just how incredible a session with Jacqueline is. I don't think there's anyone who wouldn't benefit from a chat with Jacqueline. If you're thinking about it just do it, Jacqueline and her work are worth their weight in gold."

"Jacqueline helped me to recover after a difficult time in my life. Her professional techniques and attitude are very effective. I would highly recommend her to anyone who needs to overcome psychological issues. She helped me to heal emotional trauma of the past, get rid of negative thinking, achieve more positive and hands on approach to life, improve my relationships and become more positive and assertive, and have faith in myself. She also provided me with many tools that I can apply in my future life. I cannot thank her enough!"

"Jacqueline Hurst has profoundly changed my life and given me through her guidance the opportunity to get to know myself, understand myself and love myself as a person. Her skilled work and tireless support have allowed me to embrace condition-less self-love and build up a skillset to navigate me through challenging periods. Having battled with issues for a long time, Jacqueline was the first therapist to fully understand; to fully 'get' me. She has never failed to push me just that little bit further towards myself, to a point I would have never reached without her. I fully recommend her to anyone, who really wants to change something in his life for the better."

"I have in 4/5 sessions changed my life by reaching out to someone who got me and have been able to remove any "rose tinting" that has been therefore for so long! I no longer hate my image in the mirror, I eat if I want to eat rather than feeling guilty about it and more importantly have managed to wipe off a 4-page list of negative thoughts to be left feeling my own version of normal which is great! Thank you, Jacqueline for helping me change my life."

"Jacqueline is wonderful at what she does. She helped me conquer my needle phobia & helped with some other issues in only a few sessions. She was encouraging and keen to make me a more positive and optimistic person; while being friendly and professional. I couldn't recommend her highly enough. She was a great find."

"Jacqueline Hurst is a profoundly gifted and insightful practitioner/hypnotherapist. Working with her allowed me to reframe and ultimately let go of my longstanding struggle with weight loss and problematic eating. She has an almost uncanny ability to "get it" and focus attention where it's truly needed. For the first time in many exhaustive years, I feel wonderful and in control - she has quite literally changed my life."

"I would give 6 stars but it's not an option... Because Jacqueline is one of those rare finds that will do precisely what she says on the tin. As a total cynic in life, she has helped me completely change the way I think and approach life, and the results are outstanding. Book yourself in, this woman works!"

"I engaged Jacqueline's corporate services to work with my management team, assisting them with personal development. I was a little unsure as to how they would respond to the coaching however I have been amazed at how they have reacted. In the main they are more energised and positive in their daily tasks, they are now equipped with technique's and models that help prevent stress and anxiety making them more effective in their roles. It has proved to be a very good investment for the company."

"I can whole heartedly recommend Jacqueline. After working with her for just a few weeks she managed to help me undo some negative thinking behaviours I had lived with most of my life. Jacqueline has a unique style that is totally effective; she is very intuitive and has a way of getting to the root of the issue."

"I came to Jacqueline desperately stuck, unable to break the vicious cycle of bingeing and restricting food. In a few short months this amazing woman has not only completely transformed my relationship with food but has also changed my whole perception of myself. I feel the happiest I have in a long time and can't recommend this amazing woman enough."

"It is hard to describe how helpful the work Jacqueline and I did together...it is incredible how far I have come. I stopped caring about what people thought and realised how powerful her process is in making me a positive happy and a more confident and proactive individual. I am not as affected by people's behaviour as much as I normally am. It's been life changing."

"When I first went to see Jacqueline I was quite simply, broken. After 4 years of going around in circles in therapy and 10 years of anti-depressants I'd got to a point where (I thought) I knew myself pretty well but was still totally unable to deal with any kind of perceived rejection, with work, friends, family, but most of all, relationship break-ups. After a few short months I'm truly happy and content with my life, anti-depressant free and confident, because Jacqueline has taught me the tools to cope with anything life throws my way. Her methods are dynamic and she isn't afraid to push you, but it's always done with compassion. She has an innate sense of exactly what you need and sets about getting you there as quickly as possible. Whatever your problem is, if you're ready to deal with it, I promise you - Jacqueline has the answer. She's changed my life. I can't put it any more succinctly than that."

"I actually knew from our very first session that the change was going to work - I can only describe as feeling like a switch had changed polarity - that simple and that definite. I was scared to make any predictions as being on stage is unpredictable and there was one day of wobble, but even that I dealt with in such a different way - and that was only a rehearsal, the big culminating concert that was on Saturday - the one I was holding up as the acid test, just went brilliantly. This will make such a big difference to my whole working life - wow!"

"I contacted Jacqueline after suffering a panic attack when a large spider got into my kitchen. I have had a phobia of spiders all of my life and had simply just accepted it as part of who I am but after crying all the way to work I decided that enough was enough and got in touch with Jacqueline who I knew from a previous life and I knew did work on phobias through her hypnotherapy. I had no idea what to expect when I started hypnotherapy but Jacqueline was brilliant explaining the process step by step and giving me a general idea of what to expect although everyone is different. The results have been brilliant. I have never been able to kill a spider before and been reduced to tears simply removing a dead spider but I have been able kill a spider in the kitchen since starting my sessions. More importantly I can simply walk past a spider and think 'oh, spider' without going into panic mode. The relief of no longer being afraid is incredible; I no longer have to think 'what will I do if there is a spider' because I know what I will do and that it completely down to Jacqueline and I will be eternally grateful as she has changed my life."

"Having struggled with emotional eating for as long as I can remember, I felt totally helpless when I first saw Jacqueline. We worked together through my issues in a safe and positive environment and my lifetime of destructive eating is now over! I am truly grateful to Jacqueline for her help and thoroughly recommend her to anyone in the same situation."

"Jacqueline has been a really big help. I was sceptical about hypnosis and not sure that anyone would be able to help; however, when I started I soon realised a truly positive impact on my life. I am feeling more confident, more outgoing and stopped questioning myself. The changes are continuing to happen, and she put me in the right direction. I would certainly recommend her to anyone looking for changing and bettering themselves."

"Hi Jaqueline, I never had the chance to thank you for all you did for me, there are moments where I surprise myself, especially when facing difficult situations and having the inner strength to bring back my thoughts to the right place your work is magic."

Printed in Great Britain
by Amazon